"PUT THAT

By Jayne Leaney

BASED ON A TRUE STORY ABOUT
NIPPER, WHO RESCUED 300 COWS AND
SHEEP FROM A FARM FIRE, AMONGST
OTHER HEROICS

Nipper collecting his award for' Intelligence and
Courage' from the RSPCA

Copyright © *Jayne Leaney,* 2024

All Rights Reserved

This book is subject to the condition that no part of this book is to be reproduced, transmitted in any form or means; electronic or mechanical, stored in a retrieval system, photocopied, recorded, scanned, or otherwise. Any of these actions require the proper written permission of the author.

First published in 2013 in Kindle format.

Illustrations by

Alex Slack

Preface

My name is Nipper and I live and work very hard on a sheep and cattle farm in Sussex. The story I am about to share with you covers some amusing incidents, but more importantly some traumatic events that took place back in early 1980's when a young couple called Tom and Becky came to live in the farm cottage. They brought with them a bundle of fun and trouble, who went by the name of Tina, a Collie x Labrador. She instantly became my best friend. From the day they moved in, my life changed dramatically.

My story covers all manner of my responsibilities as a farm dog, herding cattle, rounding up escapees, sheep dipping, lambing, four spoilt horses and I will enlighten you on Will the Weasel.

During Tom and Becky's stay at the cottage, I had to deal with three separate fires. The worst of these for me was the barn fire; after which, my life took an interesting turn, triggering many new adventures.

I have changed a few of the human characters and places, but all my animal friends have their true identities.

(PS: From Tom & Becky – Find out how Nipper, quite rightly, was mentioned in all the daily newspapers and won two prestigious awards for his heroics.)

Dedication

Firstly, I would like to dedicate this book to our wonderful and courageous firemen. Secondly, to our loyal and faithful dogs, working or not, who give us so much joy and friendship.

Acknowledgements

A big thank you should go to my sisters-in-law Jenny England and Lesley Cripps and my good friend Paula Cook for their proof reading skills, support and encouragement. Another big thank you to my brother, Clive England for his IT expertise and not forgetting, my husband, Patrick for his memory, brilliant ideas and all his support, especially when he had to cook dinner on a couple of occasions!

Table of Contents

Preface i

Dedication ii

Acknowledgements iii

Chapter 1: New Arrivals At Cherry Tree Farm 3rd June 1983 ... 1

Chapter 2: Meeting New Friends 6

Chapter 3: A Different Routine..................................... 18

Chapter 4: New Mates & Silly Drivers 24

Chapter 5: Sheep Dipping 30

Chapter 6: Tina's Hero 39

Chapter 7: Party Time 48

Chapter 8: The Weasel Get's It! 57

Chapter 9: Comings And Goings 68

Chapter 10: Tina Gets In A Pickle 76

Chapter 11: The Kids Come To Stay 86

Chapter 12: Lambing Time 95

Chapter 13: The Combine Harvester Fire 103

Chapter 14: The Operation! 107

Chapter 15: The House Fire 113

Chapter 16: Put That Dog Out! 123

Chapter 17: Putting Things Back Together.............. 139

Chapter 18: I'm Honoured 152

Chapter 1

New Arrivals at Cherry Tree Farm 3rd June 1983

They arrived during a storm in a tractor and trailer. I could hear the tractor pull into the drive, but I was too scared to go out of the garage and investigate. Anyway, this was a farm, it was usual to hear the tractor, but not here at the cottage. I'll go and look in a minute when the storm's over and the rain stops, but for now I'm staying put. I just hope no-one notices that I'm hiding in the garage, while the thunder and lightning crash around me and this torrential rain hammers down on the roof. To be honest, I'm trembling in terror.

I could hear them splashing around outside, rushing in and out of the cottage and the lady shouting to hurry up and get the bed in as the mattress was getting soaked. The storm rolled on and on and the rain poured down. It was going to be a long dark day, when in fact it should be warm and sunny; it was summer after all. What would these new people be like I wondered, will they let me stay in the garage, will they be kind and more importantly, will they feed me?

It wasn't long before I found out. The man came into the garage with a large box and saw me cowering and shaking in the corner. He put the box down and came over and crouched down beside me. He slowly moved his hand towards me and I smelt something familiar, but what was it? He stroked my head, "come on lad, there's nothing to be scared of, the storm will soon be over and I have someone I think you'd like to meet – I think you and Tina will be good friends, very good friends. I'll be back in a minute". With that, off he went and called out for Tina.

Well it was love at first sight – this black dog with a white star on her chest, came bounding through the door and leapt on top of me, licking my face. She danced back and forth, wagging her tail and chatting so fast "Oh delighted to meet you, I'm Tina. Who are you? Do you live here? We've just moved in. I've had a terrible day, I've been so scared. My owners packed everything in boxes and loaded them on the trailer and into the car. I've been so worried about where they were going. I was fretting they'd leave me behind like my last owners. Anyway, I'm here now and it is nice to meet you, shall we go and play outside?"

"Whoa girl, slow down. My name is Nipper and I'd rather stay here in the dry" I replied. "Maybe later, when the rain stops. To be honest, I'm a little bit scared of the thunder, but I would like to be your friend and I'm certainly up for showing you around." So Tina sat down next to me, which I found comforting. She said she'd keep me company until I felt able to go out. Actually, I think she was fed up with being told off for getting in the way and under everyone's feet, while exploring her new home. I don't think she liked being ignored while her guardians frantically tried to move all the furniture into their new home and I was certainly glad of the distraction from the storm.

It wasn't long before the rain eased up and the heavens became a lot quieter. "Come on, let's go" barked Tina, bouncing round in circles towards to the door. "The rain has stopped and I'm busting to see what's outside. I tentatively got up and sauntered to the door, whereupon the sun burst through the clouds. With that she was off, racing round the garden, nosing and sniffing every shrub and blade of grass, rolling around in the mud and as I lead the way through the gate, she leapt over the fence into the farmyard, just for the fun of it. Little did I know how she would change my life and what larks we were going to have.

We ran and ran, racing round the farmyard and fields, exploring the hedgerows for rabbits. I introduced her to the cows and the sheep. I explained to Tina about my responsibilities for keeping the animals safe, how I was always on duty and that I was relied upon, night and day, to make sure those stupid sheep stayed where they were supposed to be. I went on to tell her that they were always looking for ways to escape to a field with better grass and sometimes just escape. When we had just reached the top field, we heard her name being called in the distance. "Come on Nipper" she said as she was hurtling back towards the farm, "its dinner time".

Tina leapt through the back door and skidded across the kitchen floor, leaving a trail of mud in her wake. She then crashed into the cupboard on the other side of the room and upset her food bowl, but before anyone could moan, she was scoffing up her dinner like it was her last meal and licking the floor clean. I felt sure she would be in trouble for all that mess, but all I heard was laughter from within. The lady bent down and stroked her "what are you like young Tina? I hear you've made a new friend, what have you done with him? Tina trotted to the back door, wagged her tail, looked at me and back to the Lady. "Hello Nipper, would you like some food?" said the lady. With that she fetched another bowl and invited me in. I sat perfectly still, there was no way I was going through that door. She looked at me and then came towards me with the bowl of delicious smelling food "alright boy, that's fine, you can have yours out here, I quite understand you're a free spirit, but if you change your mind, you are always welcome in here".

Chapter 2

Meeting New Friends

At 5.30am the following morning, the back door of the cottage opened and out bounded the ever exuberant Tina. She bounded across the yard into the garage where I was just stirring, followed by the lady. "Morning Nipper, fancy a walk and showing us around" said the lady. So off we set at a great pace; Tina and I, ducking and diving, running together, up through the farmyard and out into the fields. The air was clear and fresh after the storm and apart from the birds singing, all was still, the best time of the day. The sun had already broken through and was pleasantly warm. The lady was trying her best to keep up, but we ran back and forth to check she was following us. We went up to the top field, where the views over the South Downs are spectacular in one direction and in the other you can see the whole farm and surrounding farmland. The farm was situated about 15 miles north of Brighton and just five miles north of the South Downs. It was a mile down a long lane and it seemed like we were miles from anywhere; we were in our own little world. There are woods too, which have the best smells for sniffing out deer, foxes, badgers and pheasants and best of all squirrels to chase, but for today we just explored the fields. We were out for about an hour and when we returned to the cottage, the lady again invited me in for breakfast; again I sat down outside and waited. A few moments later I heard Tina tucking into her bowl and then the lady brought a bowl of warm porridge out to me. I'd never had this before, in fact I'd never had breakfast provided before, but I soon wolfed it down and wagged my tail in gratitude - I could really get used to this.

After breakfast Tina came and lay down next to me in the sunshine and started to tell me about her life. Apparently this was her fourth home. The first was awful, they had three young children that hung onto her ears and poked and prodded her, but the worst was being locked in the kitchen for hours and hours. Then one day the owners had had enough of her chewing the kitchen chairs and ripping up the lino and shut her in the shed outside; feeding her a meagre meal once a day and only let her out in the garden for short spells. The last straw was when they let her out one day after a particularly long day in the dark shed and she growled at them - they just didn't understand that she liked to run and play and eat. So the local dog rescue centre was called. They came and bundled Tina into a van and took her back to the centre where she was again confined to a kennel, where she stayed for weeks and weeks – at least she was fed and taken for walks and she had the company of other dogs, although she could only see and chat with them. She soon learned to look longingly at every potential new owner, but if they had children with them, she sloped to the back of the Kennel until they'd passed by.

Then one Sunday afternoon she was taken for a walk and on the way back to the kennels, this tall stocky chap and his wife (and no children) came towards her – she just had an instinct about them and took a daring chance. She ran full tilt at the man and leapt up into his arms, licking his face at the same time. She nearly bowled him over. "Please, please take me home with you, I'm so bored here, I will behave, honest". The couple laughed and laughed and that was that; Tina went to her new home on a small farm surrounded by fields. Absolute heaven! The rescue centre explained that Tina was not good with children, so to be vigilant at all times with her. She needed a great deal of tender loving care and a little gentle exercise to start with and food; they suggested porridge for breakfast. She had come to them in a very poor state, almost emaciated and they had had trouble helping her gain weight as she was fretting all the time at being locked up in the kennels, but felt sure she would be ideal for them and vice versa.

Tina went on to explain that her masters were called Tom and Becky and as long as she didn't growl at anyone or chew the furniture and didn't steal any food, life was just perfect. She was now sixteen years old in dog years and all she knew was her mum was a labrador and her father was a collie, just like my handsome self, although she never met him, she apparently had characteristics just like him. She then told me how happy she was with Tom and Becky and being here. She related many tales of long walks on the downs and exploring Ashdown Forest and chasing rabbits and deer and foxes, when all of a sudden she closed her eyes and promptly went to sleep.

I must have dozed off too in the warm sun, the next thing I knew Becky and Tina were heading down the drive, "come on Nipper, we're off to meet the horses" squeaked Tina in her excitement. The horses were kept on the other side of the road down a long bumpy track at Little Orchards Farm. There was the most beautiful old cottage settled in behind the apple orchard, which was left empty most of the time. The owner of the farm had five grown up children and they used it as a holiday cottage in the summer months mainly. I loved their visits, there was always something going on, a walk or a ride out with the horses and sometimes even a party. The parties were often outside, with the barbeque going, which meant I'd have plenty to eat; I particularly loved the sausages.

To the north of the cottage was a large yard with six stables and a barn which stored hay and straw. There were several paddocks and fields surrounding the buildings; one of which had a very large and overgrown pond, which was great for cooling down in on a hot day like today.

Becky went out into the field with the horses and walked towards them as they began to wander over to meet her. Tina lay down quietly by the gate, but I raced up and down the fence, ready for action and rescue, whimpering to Becky to be careful, but she didn't seem to notice.

There were two big horses and Wills (short for Sweet William), a little black aged pony of 30 plus years, who had the kindest temperament. For years he carried all the children round, going to local gymkhanas and pony shows. He was always careful that they didn't fall off, even when jumping, he'd side step, his little legs going ten to the dozen underneath, changing direction on a sixpence, ducking and diving and often manoeuvring his head and neck to scoop them back into the saddle. He was well loved by everyone, as they all had happy memories of winning rosettes and lazy days riding round the farm. Wills was very content with life and was now enjoying his retirement, except for one thing; the poor old chap suffered with a thing called 'sweet itch'. The midges in the summer used to irritate him beyond intolerance and he rubbed and rubbed his mane on a low tree bough until it bled.

The big horses were mother and son. Chicory, the mother, a very good looking and kindly bay mare with a white blaze on her face and her beautiful mane hanging jet black below her neck. She was rather rotund and slightly aging also, after having several foals over the years, but she could still cover the ground at some speed and grace when needed. Then there was her six year old son called Toby – he was a huge 17 hands high chestnut gelding, again with a long flowing mane the colour of flaxen. He was so handsome and he knew it. There was nothing he liked more than to prance and cavort around, showing off.

He loved to gallop and buck and play, but for me he was so unpredictable and boisterous, I had to keep eyes in the back of my head whenever I was near him.

Becky had come well prepared though, with pockets full of apples, carrots and mints. She chatted away with the horses, letting them come to her and smelling all her treats. I needn't have worried, they all got on splendidly. Becky noticed that Toby had something tangled up in his tail. "Well Toby, we can't leave you in that mess, if you just stand still for a moment, I'll untangle you". So she started gently pulling the long strands of tail hair aside and little by little removed a large piece of barbed wire. I couldn't believe it, Toby standing as quiet as a mouse until she'd finished. He seemed to instantly trust her and knew she was only trying to make him comfortable. She praised him all the time for being a good boy and gave him a well-deserved mint, patting his neck, "I can see we are going to get on fine you and I", to which he gave her a gentle nudge in thanks and agreement.

As Becky turned and headed out of the field, she saw Tom coming down the track to meet them. She said to Tina and me "come on you two, you've been good too, especially as it's so warm, shall we go home and find some lunch - I'm starving" said Becky. She was right; I was getting hot under my thick shaggy coat. I knew what I needed and raced over to the pond, leapt off the bank as high as I could, tucked my legs under me and sploshed, belly first into the cool water. As my head surfaced, I could hear the roars of laughter from Tom and Becky, I knew they were thoroughly impressed with my dive; not so Tina. She trotted back and forth on the bank – "Oh Nipper, that looks like fun and I would like to cool down with you, but that's water, I'm really not sure, I can't see the bottom". Tom picked up a small stick and threw it for Tina to retrieve - her favourite game. After fetching the stick a couple of times, Tom threw it into the pond towards me, so I took it in my mouth, swam to the edge, scrambled up the bank and dropped it at Tom's feet, shaking my body from side to side, water soaking everything and everyone within six feet of me. There were squeals of joy from Tom and Becky with the shock of suddenly being sprayed with the cold water. Tom threw the stick back into the pond, so again I ran and leapt for an even more spectacular dive and as I surfaced, grabbed the stick to more howls of laughter. On the third throw, Tom teased Tina with the stick, "come on girl, your turn", but at the last second he aimed it back into the pond and before she realised what had happened, she'd was at the top of the bank, front legs in the air, heading downwards. She completely submerged under the surface; water going up her nose, as she righted herself; there was much coughing and snorting. Tom and Becky were shouting encouragement from the bank, telling her how brave and clever she was and that was that, Tina could swim. We played this game for another half an hour and then headed back to the farm for lunch.

Becky went in to prepare lunch, while Tom went into the back garden and moved an old wooden picnic bench into the shade of the apple tree. Becky brought out a tray of food with ham sandwiches for Tom and a cheese sandwich for herself, being vegetarian. There were crisps and apples and a couple of dog chews for Tina and myself.

Once lunch was over, Tina and I settled ourselves under the tree. I was just dozing off when Tina said "I've told you my history, so come on, it's your turn. How did you end up here, what's your story?" So I sat up straight and began. "I've been here as long as I can remember, at least thirty five dog years. I was brought here as a puppy. I used to live in the cottage, but as I grew up, I preferred to live outside, it was always far too hot in the cottage and as the people who lived here then had two small children, they were more than happy not to have me in the house. I never stray too far from the farm as I need to be watchful of the cows and sheep. I never know when I'm needed to round them up and move them to different pastures or help out loading them on lorries. I'm basically a free agent, happy to lend a helping hand when needed. There's not so much to do in the summer, but come the winter, its nonstop with the lambs and fetching the cows in at night.

The owners have had several jack russells over the years, all named Danny. They've always been good company when they're here, but they were only ever interested in hunting rabbits and getting into mischief, they wouldn't know how to round up sheep and certainly couldn't be trusted to do so. There are also a couple of dogs in the neighbouring garden, a black Labrador, named Lacey and a boxer called Joey. They, like you, sleep in the house at night but are kept in a large pen and kennels outside during the day. You'll meet them on walks occasionally. They're, pleasant enough, but they are always barking and posturing at me, as if they own the territory. I just ignore them and I suggest you do the same."

Becky cleared the plates away and disappeared into the kitchen. She then reappeared carrying what looked like brush, comb and scissors. "You just lie down and relax young man" she told me, "let's see if we can't tidy you up a bit and make you more comfortable". "But I am comfortable. What are you doing with those?" I fretted, but I needn't have worried, within seconds I was gently being groomed. There were handfuls of black and white clumps of my coat blowing round the lawn in the summer breeze. Becky was very careful to cut out the matted lumps and not pull at the tangles. This was a first, and boy it felt good, how relaxed was I? "There! All done! You'll have all the ladies after you now you're even more handsome" she said. I put my paw on her hand in thanks, to which she rubbed the top of my head, "no problem" she said.

Tina and I had a lazy afternoon out in the garden, while Tom and Becky were inside unpacking boxes and generally getting the house arranged for their stay. Later that afternoon, Becky came out, armed with some apples, a bottle and a head collar. "What now?" I thought, as we followed her back down to Little Orchards? She went back to the horse's field, handed out the apples and put the head collar on Wills. She opened the bottle and spread some of the contents on Wills mane and the top of his tail. "There, that should help with the midges you poor old thing".

We then had a pleasant walk round the fields and back up to Cherry Tree where Tom was waiting for us. Something caught my eye tucked in behind the garage door. "What's this?" I thought, as I wandered over for a sniff? "It's your new bed" said Tom. There was a very large and comfy looking winged armchair. "We can't fit it in the lounge and as I noticed you sleep on the ground outside, I thought you might like it for the damp days. Come on, up you get, try it for size" as he tapped the seat. He wants me up on the furniture? That's not usual, but who am I to argue. So up I jumped and padded around to test it for comfort, I flopped down and curled my tail round to my head – luxury. Becky again provided a bowl of dinner and put it down outside the door, but I didn't want to move in case they thought I didn't like my new bed – I'll have it later thanks" I replied.

Chapter 3

A Different Routine

Again next morning Becky was up at 5.30am and again Tina came bounding out ready for her walk. We charged across the garden, this time we both leapt over the garden gate, through the farmyard and away. But today, as we came round the corner of the barn, there before us was 'old Charlie fox'. Without a word to each other, we were off as fast as our legs could carry us, with only one thing on our mind. We were gone for over an hour and we honestly didn't hear Becky whistling us because the chase took us to the very top field of the farm where we then lost Charlie and his scent. We combed every inch of that field, checked every single foxhole and rabbit burrow, but to no avail; he was gone. "Come on Nipper" said Tina, "let's go home, I'm getting hungry and I think Becky might be getting worried".

I don't think Becky was too impressed with us, as she was late for work; although she did tell us we were good for coming back, you could hear the exasperation in her voice.

Once we'd had our porridge, Becky drove off and we went and found Tom up in the farmyard. He was with the farm manager, Will (or 'The Weasel' as I prefer to call him), attaching the mower to the tractor for hay cutting. It had been decided that yesterday's breeze had dried the grass enough to start making hay and as the weather prediction for the next few days was dry and sunny, they were going to go for it.

Tom greeted us, "hello you two, I hear you were not very popular on this morning's walk; off chasing foxes and ignoring your mum". Tina sidled round Tom's legs in some sort of apology, which seemed to please him, so I followed suit and did the same. I'd also rather be nearer Tom than the Weasel, as he just didn't understand me at all.

I heard Tom ask Will about me and whether it was alright to feed me and take me for walks with Tina. "Sure, that's fine; to be honest, I don't always remember to feed him every day if he's not around. He doesn't seem to like me very much. He never does anything I say and he's pretty useless with instructions; although left to his own devices, he always seems to get the job done. So yes, feel free, he seems to have taken to you".

I stood as tall as I could and glared at him "Useless with instructions? - You imbecile! If you didn't stand out in the middle of the field shouting and hollering, but just stood quietly holding the gate open, I'd know which field I was heading for and I'd have no trouble at all in moving those stupid sheep! Not to mention, embarrassing me in front of them by cursing me and taking swipes at me with your stick!" Tina came to my side. "What are you grumbling about" she said. "Oh nothing, I'll tell you later" I replied.

Tom drove off to the hay field and we ran behind the tractor, careful not to get too close to the huge back wheels. Tina and I had another look for Charlie and then settled down at the side of the field in the shade, watching Tom drive up and down. Tina asked me about the farm manager. "What was all that about earlier? What's he like? I noticed you keep your distance from him and I sensed your hackles go up when he was speaking about you" she said. "Well it's best you keep your distance from him, he's often in a bad mood and takes it out on me if things don't go exactly as he likes. Luckily I don't see too much of him and I'm a lot quicker on my feet than he is, but just be wary of him" I warned.

Later in the day Becky came home from work, quickly changed from smart clothes to shorts and T-shirt and walked us down to see the horses. This time she tied them all up to the fence, picked out their feet and groomed all three, which they all seemed to enjoy as much as I did yesterday. The whole time she was chatting away to them and in particular telling young Toby how good he was being. I think this was the first time anyone had picked his great big feet up, although he didn't seem too bothered, I stayed well alert, just in case there was any nonsense. Becky put some more stuff from the bottle on to Wills' mane and tail, gave them all mints and let them go. She then suggested we might like a swim in the pond and threw a small stick she found into the pond. Tina and I raced to the bank and in unison took off and dived into the cool water, racing to be first to find the stick – I let Tina win.

This became our regular routine and I very much appreciated the company, especially on walks, but more than anything, it was great to know when I'd be eating my next meal and such good wholesome food.

At the end of the week, when Becky came home from work to find Tina and I waiting for her, she noticed the large blue garden pots that she placed in front of the cottage were now overflowing with beautiful pink and purple petunias. "Oh how lovely, but that's odd, Tom's been hay making, he couldn't have had time to do that. I wonder who did?" she exclaimed. As she walked closer to have a look, she noticed a card sticking out from the flowers. It read:

Thought these pots looked sad and lonely,

Thought I'd fill them and make them homely!

Wishing you all the best in your new home. Love from Monica (Mon) & Joe at Sunflower Cottage.

"Well how kind is that; Monica, the next door neighbour has filled them as a welcome. Sorry Nipper, you'll have to wait a while for your walk tonight, as I better go and introduce myself and thank her – I won't be long." So Becky and Tina went next door, they were gone for ages, it seemed like hours, but eventually they returned. With them were Monica and her dogs, Lacey and Joey and Tina trotting along in between looking very pleased with herself; so we all went for our usual walk to see the horses. Lacey and Joey were actually a lot friendlier than I'd first thought. In fact they were great fun and loved to chase round in the same way as Tina and I. The two ladies were non-stop talking and let us dogs mosey about as we pleased.

Our afternoon walks became a regular feature from then on and in fact, was good news, because we often went for much longer walks and explored the huge woods further up the lane, with loads of new smells. I couldn't believe that in one week I not only had one new best friend, but three.

Chapter 4

New Mates & Silly Drivers

After our usual early morning activities, Tom, Becky and Tina went off in their car. "Won't be long Nipper, we're off to fetch Lady – you're in charge until we get back" said Tom. So I sat on the front lawn and waited. Sure enough, Tom and Tina returned shortly after and shortly after that I heard the familiar sound of a horse out on the lane, heading our way. Tina ran out to meet Becky who was riding the prettiest pony I'd ever seen. She was palomino in colour with the longest and loveliest flaxen mane and tail. She held her head high, looking inquisitively at her new surroundings. They turned down the track to Little Orchards, so I ran to join them.

About half way down, Toby, Chicory and Wills heard Lady's arrival. They rushed over to the gate and whinnied their greeting, to which Lady whinnied in reply and started dancing about. I have to say, she looked wonderful, as she arched her neck and held her tail high, doing an exaggerated slow motion trot and at the same time floating in mid-air; a real show off. The excitement of all the horses was obvious. Becky patted Lady's neck and jumped off as they arrived at the field gate. Lady squealed with delight as Toby nuzzled into her mane over the gate and Chicory touched her nose in greeting.

Becky quickly took Lady's saddle off and gave her and the others some mints, "right you guys, you've all got to behave yourselves, especially you Toby. Treat Lady gently, she's so much smaller than you and things will be just fine" she said. She led Lady through the gate and undid her bridle, as she slipped it over her head; all four were off at a flat out gallop, squealing again with delight as they went. Even Wills seemed keen to kick up his heels and prance about, showing he was still up for it.

Tina, Becky and I stood by the gate for nearly an hour, while the horses raced round, this way and that, bucking and prancing, then skidding to a dead halt to nuzzle each other in a proper introduction and then off again for a gallop. Eventually, they'd all worn themselves out and decided to put their heads down in the long grass to eat. Lady wandered over to Becky and gave her a nudge as if to reassure her that she would be fine here in her new home and that she was happy with her new mates. She then went over to the trough for a drink and headed back over to the others for more grass.

Becky seemed happy that the horses would settle down and before long become good friends, so we returned to the cottage, where Tom and the Weasel were sitting in the kitchen drinking coffee. I lay down on the front lawn, where I could just hear them chatting in the kitchen and Becky preparing lunch; I must have nodded off. The next thing I remember, I was startled by a loud bang, metal on metal. I jumped up and saw two cars concertinaed in front of me, one of which was billowing smoke. I barked and I barked again. "Come on, someone, anyone, please come, these people need help". I ran to the back door and barked again, then ran back to the front barking all the way.

Tom was first on the scene, followed hastily by Becky and the Weasel. Tom quickly assessed the damage to the cars and headed straight to the car that was smoking from the bonnet, at the same time shouting to Becky to phone for an ambulance. He opened the car door and spoke to the driver, reassuring her that help was on the way. He turned off the ignition and asked Will to go and fetch a fire extinguisher from the farm. The driver of the other car, a young lad of about 18; although looking shaky, had managed to climb out of his car and limp up the small bank and sit down. Becky returned and reported that the police and an ambulance were on their way. It wasn't long at all before I could just hear a siren in the distance. The Weasel raced back with the extinguisher, but it was decided not to use it as the car had stopped smoking. Tom was struggling to get the driver's seatbelt off; the whole time chatting away to an attractive and well-dressed lady.

The police arrived first, followed a couple of minutes later by the ambulance. In the meantime Tom had somehow managed to free the lady's seatbelt and move her seat back in her car. I knew she was hurt quite badly, apart from her crying out in pain, I could smell blood. The police and ambulance men were marvellous; it didn't take long before they slowly manoeuvred her out and had her on a stretcher and in the back of the ambulance. Poor lady had smashed both her knees into the dashboard.

While Tom, Becky and Will were chatting to the police, Tina came and found me. "Here Nipper, do you want a pate sandwich? They were left on the kitchen table and are quite delicious, but I really can't eat any more" she mumbled with her mouth full and dropped the sandwich at my feet. I wolfed it down in one. I was actually quite hungry; with all this excitement today my appetite had improved no end.

The police had finished taking statements and helped by Tom and Will, moved the cars off the nasty bend and onto the cottage drive to await collection from an accident recovery lorry. Both cars looked un-driveable and apparently were later written off. Tom, Becky and Will returned to the cottage. Becky bent down and rubbed me gentle behind the ears "what a clever boy you are, that's the first time I've heard you bark. We didn't hear the crash at all with the kettle and radio on and we were talking."

The next thing I heard was a very cross sounding voice from the Weasel. "Your dog has eaten my lunch!" Becky quickly ran into the kitchen "Oh, I'm sorry, I'll soon sort that out, as she grabbed the bread and looked at Tina; saying in a cheery tone, "Tina, you naughty girl! Oh, well, our fault for leaving food on the table – you don't miss a trick do you!" I was very grateful to Tina for not mentioning that I'd actually had some too.

Chapter 5

Sheep Dipping

It was going to be a very hot weekend, it was already warm and it was only 8am. Tom and Will took me out to the sheep field where I raced off round the edge of the field along the hedgerow and gathered up the sheep. They seemed to know something nasty was going to happen and were particularly difficult and stupid today. I'd just got them heading back towards the farm; all was going great and then half of them spun round and ran in the opposite direction. So I swung back and gathered them up again and then another few broke away on my blind side. Eventually though, with Tom's help and not the Weasel's hollering, we managed to shut them in the barn.

I was very hot and bothered by the end of it and needed a drink. I went over to the trough and had some water. Actually, this looks inviting, I thought, so I jumped in the trough and lay down to cool off – bliss! I then heard Tom chuckling and as I turned to look at him, he was looking at me. What's he laughing at I wondered? "Oh Nipper, I wish I had a camera with me. You certainly know how to look after yourself" he said, still chuckling away.

Shortly afterwards, Tom and Will started herding the sheep towards the small pen they had set up. They manoeuvred one of the sheep into the pen and Tom skilfully turned the sheep onto its back and Will started to trim its hooves. It was wriggling and struggling to get up, but Tom had a firm grip. Once all four hooves were clipped and tidied up, Tom let it up, but held on. Will then clipped all the wool from around the tail area. The sheep was then let through into a bigger pen, where it rushed over the far side. "One down, one hundred and ninety nine to go" said Will. It was going to be a long day.

As soon as I worked out what they had planned, I jumped over the fence to be in with the sheep and gently coaxed the sheep forward to the pen. Each time they let a sheep through to the bigger pen; I'd singled out the next one and was ready to push her through into the holding pen with Tom and Will. Tom was most appreciative and told me what a good boy I was. "That's a cracking dog" said Tom. "I don't know who trained him, but I've never seen a sheepdog do that before with no instruction. I know collies love to round up anything and everything, but that's amazing. Nipper has watched us for five minutes and sussed out what needs to be done. That will save us a lot of time, if he is going to pass sheep through to us". Will had to agree that it was quite impressive. "Actually" said Will, "I don't believe he ever had any proper training. As I said before, he always seems to get the job done somehow. To be honest, he's never been this helpful with me before". I thought to myself, you never ask nicely and I certainly wouldn't go out of my way to be helpful to you anyway, but Tom is always kind and praises me.

After the first hundred had been done, Tom and Will headed down to the cottage for a cup of tea and an early lunch. "You're back early" said Becky. I then heard Tom reporting to her how impressed he was with me, as Tina rushed out and as usual bounced around me, licking my face. "Oh, I've missed you. What have you been up to? Where have you been? I'm bored!" I told her I'd had to work and that I had an important part in this morning's proceedings and explained to her about the system I'd set up with Tom and Will. I think she was also suitably impressed too.

Becky brought out two bowls of cereal and milk for Tina and I, which was so refreshing; it hardly touched the floor before we'd both lapped it up. "I hear you've been showing off your skills again young Nipper. You'll have to teach Tina how you do it; although, perhaps, she's a bit too boisterous around the sheep." I would definitely agree with that.

After I'd had a short nap, Tom and Will reappeared. "Come on Nipper, let's get the rest of these sheep done". We carried on in the same fashion in the afternoon. Tom and Will took it in turns to upturn the sheep with the other one clipping. Becky turned up a little later with a flask of tea and some cake, but secretly, I believe she wanted to come and see me work; I could feel her eyes on the back of my head.

Once all the sheep were neat and tidy, Tom and Will bedded them down for the night, with fresh water, food and plenty of hay. Tomorrow was sheep dipping day, so the sheep were being kept in for the night so we could get an early start. It was not only our sheep that had to be dipped, but several neighbouring farms brought their sheep in to dip. Some had a dozen or so, others a few more and one lady up the lane had a couple she used as lawn mowers; trouble was they ate most of her garden plants too!

It was just getting dark when I wandered up to the farm to check the sheep were behaving themselves. I thought I'd heard them moving around. I was right – they had managed to push the gate open and had legged it back to the field. As you know, if one goes, they all go. I knew exactly which field they'd be in and headed off after them. You just can't trust them; you take your eyes off them for a minute and they do something stupid. They had a lovely cosy bed, plenty of food, but no, they have to go wandering off where they shouldn't be.

It wasn't long before I found them. I barked my irritation at them and set off quickly to the right to keep them up near the hedge; I could use that as a guide to hustle them back to the farm. All in all it took about fifteen minutes to herd them back into barn; they ran up to the far corner, swung round and came back to face me, bleating on at me for bringing them back. A few at the front stamped their feet and glared at me. I just sat down in the open gate, barked loudly at them and glared back – you stupid sheep are going nowhere else tonight.

Tom and Becky had seen the sheep file past back to the farm from their kitchen window. They switched the outside light on and came up to the farm. "Good boy, we heard you barking and wondered what was going on – we knew something must be up; we've learnt that you only bark for good reason" they were both saying together. Tom suggested someone could not have shut the gate properly when they'd left for the evening and the sheep must have pushed it open.

Tom and Becky said "goodnight" to me as they headed off to bed. I heard Becky saying to Tom how amazed she was that I could round up 200 sheep on my own and put them back through that small gap in the gate – they could have shot past and gone round and round the farm. It's as if they know, Nipper is guarding them and he won't stand any nonsense. Tom agreed. I lay down and slept the rest of the night with one eye open.

After I'd had my morning porridge and charge round the garden with Tina, Tom and I went off to work and Becky and Tina went off to see the horses. Tina wanted to come with me, until she realised Becky was going riding. She would have been bored sitting around while the sheep were being dipped and no doubt would have caused some sort of mischief.

"I'll see you later" she squeaked as she raced off with Becky.

Will had already put the chemicals in the dip, as Tom and I arrived. Tom told Will about my heroics of retrieving the sheep in the night. Will went a little red faced; "Oh, I think I was the last one out of the gate; that must have been me". You Weasel. No 'sorry' or 'thank you' or 'good boy' I thought to myself; but Tom seemed to sense what I was thinking and gave me a pat on the head.

"Well I think we're ready for the off. Tom do you want to send the sheep up the ramp and I'll push them through the dip" said Will? "Yup, that's fine with me" was the reply. Tom grabbed the nearest sheep and steered her towards the ramp as I trotted back and forth, pushing the sheep towards Tom. We soon had a system going, in the same way as yesterday. The sheep didn't like the smell of the dip. Once they'd reached the top of the ramp, they tried to turn tail, but there was no room to turn – they had to go forward. Will also was grabbing them by the scruff of the neck and dragging them into the water, before they had a chance to retreat.

Tom noticed Will put his foot on the sheep's heads and push them under the water. This caused them to cough and splutter when they came up for air, as they'd gulped in water or it had gone up their nostrils. He was not happy about this, but not sure whether to say anything. As he had only been in the job a couple of weeks, he thought he'd better hold his tongue.

To be fair to those stupid sheep, I wouldn't want to go through the dip; it did smell quite disgusting and the chemicals did sting your eyes a bit too. But, we had a job to do and Tom and Will wouldn't be doing this for the fun of it. The dip was to stop the sheep getting 'fly strike' and 'scab'. Apparently, Will designed and built the sheep dip out of an old trailer and a few redundant farm parts. The sheep walked up a narrow ramp, dropped into the water, walked or swam three or four feet, jumped out and went down a ramp the other side into a holding pen.

About half of the sheep had gone through when Becky turned up after riding. "Can I help?" she asked Tom. "Yes, I think the sheep might prefer it if you put them through the dip – try and send them in head first" he whispered to Becky. She nodded to Tom and climbed up onto the trailer with Will. "Do you mind if I have a go?" she asked Will, but before he could answer, she took firm hold of the next sheep on either side of its shoulder and pushed the sheep in head first. "Have you done this before?" asked Will, looking a bit perplexed that Becky had managed to haul the sheep in with relative ease. "Oh yes, many times. I used to help out on the farm where I kept Lady. The farmer used to give me bales of hay or straw as payment, which suited me fine". Becky winked at

Tom behind Will's back, smiling to herself. She loved working with the men, especially, when she knew she could manage the job as well as them; she also knew that Tom appreciated the help.

Chapter 6

Tina's Hero

Several weeks passed with us all settling into our new routines, regular walks with Joey and Lacey; and now riding out with Becky on Lady and Mon on her pony, Califfe, whenever they rode round the farm. Tina and I were not allowed to go on the road rides, although we often tried to sneak along, but were always caught and sent home.

There were several visitors to the cottage to see Becky and Tom's new home. I was always introduced as their and Tina's new friend and took full advantage of all the stroking and ear tickling. Tom and Becky seemed to be pleased with me and I hope they realised the feeling was mutual.

Tom's parents had come for afternoon tea and after playing ball with Tina and I, sat out in the garden, chatting and laughing. Tina and I sat either side of Tom's Mum; Tina had a real soft spot for her, as she had stayed there for several weeks during the day when she first moved in with Tom and Becky. The initial plan was for Tina to go to work with Tom on another farm, but she picked a fight with the farm Doberman and a large Old English sheepdog. The farm owner was not best pleased and told Tom that Tina was not welcome. So Tom's Mum stepped in and offered to look after her during the day, where she was spoilt rotten by the sounds of things. Becky would go and collect her after work and take her home and then out for a long walk.

I understood immediately why Tina loved her so much; she kept passing sandwich corners and other delicacies under the table to Tina and I. She also chatted to us and told me how handsome I was and had a particularly nice way of stroking my head and scratching me behind my ears.

Becky was telling her mother-in-law all about me and what a good and calming influence I was on Tina. She and Tom were so thrilled that Tina and I had become such good friends, as was I.

Once the food was finished with, Tina and I wandered off to the sit in the shade and after a short while dozed off. I was suddenly awakened by a loud yelp and a lot of growling. There was quite a commotion going on next door. I jumped up and headed towards Joey and Lacey's garden and barked that I was on my way. Mon and her husband, Joe were shouting and screaming at something light in colour, moving rather fast on the other side of the hedge.

Once the shouting had stopped, we could all hear one of the dogs whimpering in pain. Tom shouted over the hedge to the neighbours to ask what on earth was going on and were they alright; could he help? Joe called back that a large yellow Labrador had just come through the hedge from the farm and attacked Joey and Lacey – they needed to go to the vets post haste. Joey had a terrible bite to his head and Lacey was bleeding badly from a front leg. We then heard them drive off.

Tom ran up to the farm to find the man who was sorting out the new silage pit with his huge digger. He'd met the Labrador, Buster, when the man turned up for work this morning and let his dog out of the Landover. The dog ran off and the man seemed happy he was un-supervised. Tom told us later he had instantly taken a dislike to the dog, "he was a big bruiser", as he put it and seemed to be rather too sure of himself - I can vouch for that. I thought I better follow Tom and make sure he was protected.

While Tom and I were gone, Buster had doubled back and gone through the open gate into the garden. I heard Tina bark, then growl. Buster headed straight for the kitchen, which was too much for Tina, this was her house and she was going to protect it. She ran up behind him and grabbed hold of Buster's back leg as he went through the back door and tried to drag him out of her house, but he wriggled free and turned on her. I raced back to her as fast as my legs would carry me. I passed Becky and Tom's Mum, as they were racing to help Tina, who was now, to my horror, lying on her back with Buster at her throat. She was screaming, as Buster shook her like a rag doll. I saw red - without thinking I leapt through the door and bowled him over. Before he had time to move, I was on him and grabbed his ear and held on for dear life. I headed towards the back door with his ear firmly in my grasp. He put up some resistance, but ears are very tender; I gave him no choice, he was coming with me.

As soon as we were outside, Tina ran round behind him and grabbed his hind leg again. I could sense she was very frightened of this thug, but she was not going to let go. Buster was a strong dog and put up quite a fight. He dragged both Tina and I round the garden, but we held our grip on him. We were being barged this way and that, spinning in circles, all the time moving away from Becky who was trying her best to keep up, in the hopes of grabbing Buster. We were all growling with as much ferocity as we could. It seemed to go on forever, but eventually, Buster realised he'd met his match. We'd worn him down; his back legs buckled and he crashed to the ground and started to whimper. Luckily for him, his owner turned up with Tom, who caught him by the scruff of the neck and pulled him away. "I suggest you check your dog over and don't bring him back here in future" said Tom to the man. The man apologised and said he would pop round to the neighbours and sort out any vet bills. He quickly disappeared up the garden, rather red faced, scolding Buster as he went.

Tina came straight to my side and licked my face "Oh, thank you Nipper, my hero. I thought he was going to kill me, I was really scared. He was so strong and all those teeth; you were so brave". Tom and

Becky came and checked us over. There was much concern for us, but we were fine. "You brave boy", said Becky, "and you Tina. What a very nasty dog that was, but I think all that noise has upset you more than anything". Tina went very quiet for a while; I think she was very shocked. This had never happened to her before. Tom's Mum and Dad made much of us too. I heard Tom's Mum say "I thought Nipper wouldn't go in the house". "Well, it looks like he will for Tina", replied Becky. With that she popped into the kitchen and came back out with a couple of cold cooked sausages for us.

We later found out that poor Lacey and Joey had both had to have stitches in their wounds, so I think Tina and I got off very lightly indeed. We didn't see them for a couple of days.

The next morning I awoke around 4am to the most delightful scent. I slowly slid off my armchair and touched down on the concrete floor. I was very stiff from all that carry on with Buster the previous day, but my instincts took over and I soon forgot my aches. I stepped outside the garage, had a stretch and a yawn and took a good sniff of air. This smell definitely needs investigation I thought. I trotted off up the lane and before long I was up on the main road. Luckily at this time in the morning there are not too many cars about, but I had to have my wits about me. The scent was a lot stronger up here on the top of the hill. I trotted down the main road for about a mile, following my nose. A car came up from behind and slowed down, it then went passed me and pulled up in front and stopped. The door opened, but as the driver started to climb out, I quickly swung left and scrambled through the hedge and set off at a gallop across the field.

On the other side of the field was a farmhouse with several outbuildings, a big barn and some kennels. As I reached the kennels, panting slightly, I found want I was looking for. Three lovely lady collies, all looking just like me. The lady on the left came out of her kennel and stuck her nose up to the mesh to greet me. "Nice to see you again Nipper" she squeaked. "Hello Jess, how have you been keeping?" I replied. I trotted away in a circle, keeping my eyes glued on the top of the fence, I raced forward and leapt. I didn't manage it in one, but my front claws caught in the mesh and I somehow scrambled over.

The farmer was not too pleased to find me in his kennels later that morning with his favourite working dog. I usually had the strength to jump back out after my visit, but my front shoulder was still sore after the fight yesterday. I'd been well and truly caught. He put a lead rope on me and lifted me into the back of his car. I was, to be frank, very nervous of what was going to happen to me, but I was so exhausted. I thought I better go with him quietly and as he'd put a rope on me, I didn't seem to have much choice. The man said it was the dog pound for me, whatever that was.

Meanwhile, unbeknown to me, Tom and Becky had also got up earlier than normal this morning and were really worried when they found I was not in my armchair. They and Tina were frantically searching round the garden and farm, wondering if I had actually been seriously hurt in the fight the day before and they'd missed the signs.

After searching for a couple of hours, they rang the local police station and reported me as missing; in the hopes I'd been handed in. They also rang the local vets in case someone had taken me there. It wasn't long before the police phoned back and told them that a local farmer had brought me in to the police station.

To my sheer delight Becky turned up to collect me. I ran round in circles with pleasure at seeing her and couldn't help myself from squeaking my thanks. The policeman told Becky where I had been found and that the farmer was a kind gentleman. He was a little upset though, that I had probably mated with his eldest dog, Jess and she would have to go to the vets and have an injection to stop her having puppies. The policeman suggested Becky might like to give him a call and perhaps offer to pay the vets bill. She took the farmer's number and thanked the policeman for looking after me. He then told Becky "as much as he is a lovely dog, we are all glad you've come to collect him. He has been howling ever since he arrived. We've tried everything we could think of to shut him up; a short walk round the park, food, sweet talk, cuddles; I was just about to send someone out for some earplugs!"

Becky led me out to the car and opened the back door "in you pop, you rascal; we were so worried about you and there you were off enjoying yourself, doing what comes naturally". She rubbed my ears and gave me a hug. "Tina will be pleased to see you and I expect you're pretty hungry after your little adventure". I was delighted to be going home. I don't like being locked up and I don't particularly like travelling in cars. I howled all the way home, even when Becky joked to "quieten down in the back" and laughed. "We'll be home in a jiffy"; which we were.

Later in the day Becky told me she was off to see the farmer and that I'd cost her a vets bill and a bottle of wine as an apology for the inconvenience of my romancing.

Chapter 7

Party Time

The first mention I heard of a party was after our morning walk. Tina and I had been chasing foxes and had rolled in something that smelt delightful. If you smell like a fox, it's easier to sneak up on them. Becky, unfortunately, did not find the smell so appealing; especially when Tina lived in the house with her. The other problem was that Becky and Tom had the day off and decided it was bath time. Well, I must say the warm water in the old tin bath was fine, but when Tom produced a bottle of shampoo and started applying it, I was not too happy; in fact most indignant. I was having none of it – I'm not a stupid sheep and don't wish to be treated like one. I tried to leap out of the bath, but Tom had quite a firm hold on me and told me to stay still. "I won't be a minute Nipper, but we really must rinse you off. You can't go round looking like a scarecrow and smelling like a skunk. We've got a hundred people turning up for a party tomorrow – you need to be looking your best". "I back chatted that I was quite happy with the way I looked and smelt and I most definitely don't like all these bubbles". With that, I struggled even more and managed to upend the bath; tipping all the water into Tom's lap. Whoops! I quickly trotted a few paces away from him, thinking I was in real trouble. I then shook my whole body; the soap suds went everywhere. Now I really must be in trouble; I've managed to soak not only Tom, but covered both him, Becky and Tina in soap bubbles. I needn't have worried; they as usual, found it hilarious. I carried on shaking, at the same time moving away from them, just in case they decided to have another go.

Unfortunately, Tom followed me and started to call me back to him. "Nipper, come here boy, I've got a good idea. If you don't like the bath, how about rinsing you off in the trough. I know you don't mind jumping in there." He went over to it and called me again. "Come on, in you pop; we'll soon get rid of the soap and then you can go and dry off". I had to agree this was the better option, so I obliged and jumped in and Tom quickly rinsed me off. Tom told me what a good boy I was and then let me jump out. I have to say, I took great delight in soaking him further when I had another go at shaking myself dry.

It was now Tina's turn. Becky had refilled the tin bath and Tina was asked to jump in, which she did willingly. Becky worked quickly to lather her up and then washed her off with a bucket of warm water. It all took a couple of minutes and Tina looked like she was really enjoying the whole process, especially the towelling down afterwards. After Tom had cleaned out the trough and refilled it, we returned to the garden to watch Tina being dried off. She told me when it was over, it was better just to oblige; it's not so bad when you get used to it and it doesn't take long to smell doggy again.

After I'd dried off in the sun, Becky got the brushes out and began gently grooming me. She painstakingly pulled the knots apart and snipped of the really matted bits. Once again, my coat was blowing all around the garden. "There!" she said, looking pleased with herself, "very presentable; the finest looking dog in town". I looked down at my once dirty cream coloured chest and paws. I was horrified, it was now brilliant white. How on earth are my girlfriends in the village going to recognise me now? – I not only smell different, I look different too!

Tom and Becky had been in the cottage for just over a month and decided to have a party for Tom's birthday. Friends and family started turning up during the morning, armed with tents and gazebos. This all coincided with Richard, the eldest son of the farmer, visiting for the weekend. I recognised his car immediately and trotted over to him; as he headed towards me. He made a real fuss of me. I wagged my tail in mutual greeting. Tina rushed over and started barking at him, but I told her there was no need. "Richard's a good friend, he won't hurt you". So she got in on the act and Richard made a fuss of her too.

He called out "hello" to Tom and Becky. "Anything, I can do to help? – I'm at your service all day and I'm really looking forward to tonight. It's really kind of you to invite me and some of my friends" said Richard. "No problem, it's lovely to have you here. The more the merrier" replied Becky. "Fancy a bacon sandwich, before we put you to work?"

There was a real buzz going on all day, people coming and going, chatter and laughter from everyone and it wasn't long before all the tents were in place and the food laid out on the tables in one of the gazebos. Another held all the drinks, set up on a trestle table with table cloths and a large barrel of beer at one end and a big bowl of punch taking centre stage. Tom and Richard hung up some pretty coloured lights and Becky moved all the garden pots with flowers around the guy ropes and tent pegs, in the hope that people wouldn't trip up.

Tom had also been cooking a hog roast, which Tina and I had been drooling over for the last four hours, but every time we went near, we were told in no uncertain terms to "Clear Off!"

Early evening and cars started to arrive on mass. A car park had been set up in the farmyard and a portable toilet had been hired for the ladies and placed in the corner of the barn. I had a lot of running round to do. I needed to check everybody in and keep an eye on things, but there were so many of them; I was having trouble keeping up. Then there was an almighty thudding noise. What on earth was going on; this needed investigation. In one of the tents was a huge booming box and to my amazement, several ladies, including Becky dancing round, arms and legs all over the place, singing and shouting, but they looked like they were enjoying themselves.

Later on Tom called out that hog roast was ready. He and Richard had lifted it off the spit onto a table and had started carving it; the smell was mouth-watering. Tom pulled off the outer skin, which he then broke up into small pieces and put on a plate, except for a couple of bits which he threw to Tina and I "careful, its hot" he told us. Becky then walked amongst the guests offering the plate "crackling anyone?" she called out. Tina and I scoffed our crackling down and went straight back to the table, but everyone was hot on our heels, armed with plates and bread rolls. You would think it was the last meal they were going to have as they pushed and shoved Tina and I out of the way. We tried to get Tom's attention by dancing round and Tina even barked at him "don't forget us, we're really hungry too". Tom acknowledged her "alright girl, you'll get some more, but you'll have to wait your turn – don't tell anyone, but I've saved you the best bits".

Once everyone had been fed; several going back two or three times for more; I watched Tina going round the straw bales people were sitting on and nudging them. "Anything for me please?" she asked, giving them her cutest look. This seemed to be working, she was being hand fed all sorts of food and if they didn't give her anything, she waited until they were distracted and helped herself. What I failed to notice, was her helping herself to their beer. I quickly joined her and stuck close to her side. I've never been so spoilt for food and attention. Everyone was chatting to us and stroking us, it was just a great evening.

After a while, I watched Tina stagger over to Becky and touch her side, there was something wrong, she was wobbling all over the place completely jelly legged. She looked up into Becky's eyes and sat down, or rather fell down in a heap. Becky gasped "what's wrong Tina?", but as she said it, Becky had worked out the problem. She rushed round to all the guests, asking them to pick their glasses up of the floor; "Oh, it's my fault, I didn't think. Tina's been helping herself to your beer and I suspect she is now feeling rather worse for wear". Tina curled up where she lay. "I'm so sorry Tina, you might be happy now, but you're going to feel rotten in the morning" said Becky, stroking her head. I'm glad now I hadn't had any, it smelt pretty awful anyway.

Several hours later, people did eventually start to disappear, some wandering up through the farm to find their cars, some crawling into their tents in the garden. I was really tired, I could hardly keep my eyes open, but I thought I'd better stay awake until they'd all settled for the night. I managed another half hour, but when I thought I really needed to sleep, I went to look for Tina to let her know I was going to bed. I found her lying by the hog roast spit, keeping warm by the fire. I told her I was off to bed, but all I got back from her was a groan, so I wandered down to the garage and climbed onto my armchair. I curled up and went into a blissful sleep.

The birds woke me as usual in the morning, but I just stayed curled up; I really was tired and I couldn't hear anybody about outside. I thought I'd have a little lie in. I awoke again about an hour later and after having a yawn and a stretch, I gently eased myself down to the ground. My porridge had usually arrived by now, but there was no sign of Tina or Becky, so I quietly walked round the garden to see if I could find them. As I checked all the tents, I could hear people breathing inside, some of them even snoring. I could only assume they must be in the cottage and still asleep. I wandered off to check the stupid sheep, make sure they were where they were supposed to be. I checked on the cattle too and returned to the cottage, where a wonderful aroma of bacon was cooking.

Tom and Becky were up now and Tom had started tidying up the garden with some of the other guests helping, but there was no sign of Tina. "Don't look so worried Nipper" said Becky, "I haven't forgotten your porridge, as she placed it in front of me. "How are you feeling this morning? You look a little brighter than Tina, but hopefully, once she's had some breakfast, she will feel up for some fresh air." It wasn't long before Tina came to the back door, but I could see she wasn't herself. She gingerly stepped out into the garden and still looked a bit unsteady on her legs. I've never seen her like this before; I couldn't understand what was wrong with her.

Becky brought out a tray with several mugs of tea, followed by a huge plate of bacon sandwiches for the remaining friends and a marmalade sandwich for herself. They all sat down for an alfresco breakfast. Tina stood near one of the straw bales and to everyone's amusement, leant on the side of it to help keep her upright. "Don't laugh" said Becky, "I feel really bad that she's got a hangover."

The friends were all chatting about the party last night and what a good time they'd had, when Tom interrupted them and said "look at Tina, she seems to have perked up a bit. Not content with stealing beer, she's now drinking my tea".

Chapter 8

The Weasel Gets It!

The last job for this Friday afternoon was to bring the bullocks back to the farm. Will was waiting by the Landover as Tom and I went to meet him. As we arrived, Will came over to me; he took me totally by surprise as he lunged at me, grabbed my back with both hands; one on my neck and one on my back. He hauled me off the ground and threw me into the back of the Landover, taking out great clumps of my coat. I've never felt pain like it - I yelped twice, actually it was more of a scream. "The Weasel! - How could he? That really hurt, firstly having my skin pinched and yanked away from my body and then landing hard on the metal floor" I cursed. The next thing that happened took my mind off my pain. Tom jumped towards Will and growled in his face "Will - what on earth did you do that for?! That's no way to pick up a dog! If you'd have bothered to open the door, Nipper would have jumped in." All the Weasel could mumble back was "oh he's fine, don't fuss".

Tom quickly came over and rubbed my neck and back. "I'm sorry about that Nipper, I had no idea he was going to do that – are you alright?" I placed my paw on his hand and tried to give a look of thanks for caring. "I'd better go and get in the front before we upset him further" Tom whispered to me.

We headed off in the Landover across the fields, up to one of the top fields where the grass is very lush and the bullocks had been fattening up for the last couple of months. Will pulled up at the gate and I jumped out of the back and rushed round to the gate, where Tom followed me – I just wanted to get away from Will. Once through the gate, Tom stroked me again and instructed me "Go do your stuff boy, fetch the cows in", but I was already off and running. As usual, I ran as fast as my legs could carry me, round the outside of the field. As I approached the bullocks, I slowed down so I didn't spook them. They were a fine looking bunch of Sussex beefers. Their coats were really shining dark red in the sunshine. As soon as they realised I was there, they spun round to watch my every move, some looking anxious. A couple of them snorted and came forward. There were 28 in all.

I circled round to the right, as Tom headed off to the left along the fence. The bullocks didn't know which way to look, but I could tell they were worried. As Tom and I neared each other, the bullocks turned and headed down the field, so Tom backed off. I trotted slowly, weaving from side to side behind them to encourage them to keep moving forwards. Sussex cows are generally nice natured and they soon worked out what I expected of them. Will drove the Landover in front and Tom and I walked at a leisurely pace behind the bullocks, occasionally changing direction, or jogging a little bit to keep them moving forward along the fence line.

Once back at the farmyard, we left them in the field next to the cottage, where they were going to spend the weekend. The day's work done, Tom headed off to the cottage and called me to him. As we approached, I could see Becky gardening out in the front, with Tina lying by her side. I ran down to tell Tina what had happened to me and hopefully get some sympathy, but before I could get the words out, Tom started telling Becky what the Weasel had done and he sounded really cross. "No! Poor Nipper; I'd have hit him if I'd been there" Becky cried and I believe she would have too. She looked really upset; "come here mate, what a nasty man; how could he?" She gave me a big hug and gently stroked my sore back. Tina pushed her way in and sat down next to Becky; I think she was a little jealous I was receiving so much fuss, but she didn't say so.

Next morning after Tom and I had checked the bullocks and the sheep, Tom and Becky headed down to Little Orchards to see the horses; apparently Becky had a surprise for Tom. Tina and I were hot on their heels and once we knew where we were going, we ran on ahead. It was fairly unusual for Tom to accompany us, but I soon found out why. Becky put head collars on Toby and Lady and led them into the yard. She soon had them groomed off and then put a bridle on Toby, followed by a saddle. As usual, she chatted all the time, putting the horses at their ease. She then led Toby over to the mounting block and asked Tom to stroke his neck. Before I could blink and to my amazement she was sitting on top of him. I wasn't sure this was such a good idea. Toby was so big and certainly the most boisterous of all the horses.

I don't think Tom was too happy about it either. "I realise I can't dissuade you, but please be careful. You don't know him very well yet and the ground is very hard" he warned Becky. "Trust me Tom" she replied. "If I can't show Toby trust, how on earth is he going to trust me – we'll be fine."

She asked Toby to walk on and gently squeezed her heels into his side in encouragement. Toby duly stepped forward and walked round the yard looking quite pleased with himself. They went round a couple of times and Becky patted his neck and told him what a good boy he was. She then swung her leg over his back and landed softly on the ground next to him. "That's enough for your first ride" she told him as she threw her arms round his neck and gave him some mints. She told Tom she'd been doing a little more with him each day and had been lying over his back for the last few days when he was standing near the gate. I could see Becky was really excited and pleased with herself.

On the way back up to the cottage, Becky asked Tom if he would come back down tomorrow morning and perhaps they could go a little further. So we did the same again the following morning, but this time Becky and Toby headed off up the farm track and Tom lead Lady behind. Toby carried his head and tail up high, ears pricked forward and I have to say, he looked quite handsome as he marched off. Once we'd reached the lane, Becky asked Toby to "whoa up", which he did instantly and Tom brought Lady to stand next to him. He seemed to be quite pleased to be out; I don't remember him ever leaving the field before and considering he was now six years old, I thought he might be either very excited or very scared. I needn't have worried, with Becky in charge and Lady for company; he looked full of confidence and just pleased to see the other side of the hedge.

Becky and Toby stood there for a good five minutes until a car went passed. Becky praised him up and then turned him back down the track. "You brilliant horse, you are so brave" she chirped. Tom seemed a little more relaxed now that he'd seen Toby walk quietly up the lane and stand still for the car to pass. "You were right" he said to Becky. "He certainly does seem to have put his trust in you and perhaps Lady. Maybe he was just trying to impress her. I've noticed them together a lot in the field, they seem to have become good friends".

"I'm just so excited" said Becky, as we wandered back to the cottage. "There is a real thrill for me being the first one on his back and it hasn't taken long at all. It certainly won't be long before we can go out for proper rides, but I'll have to make sure Lady doesn't get jealous. She's my first love and always will be".

A little later Tom and Becky had changed into smarter clothes and drove off with Tina to Tom's Mum and Dad's for lunch they told me as they were leaving. "We won't be long Nipper" said Tom through the car window. They must have passed the Weasel up the lane on their way out, as he pulled into the farm shortly after they'd left. I hoped he hadn't seen me as I slunk off to the back garden to lie down in the shade and wait for Tina to come home. I saw him go into the farm office and I wondered what he was doing here on a Sunday afternoon.

A couple of hours later I heard Will shouting my name. "Oh no, what does he want?" I thought, as I ventured round the side of the cottage to see what all the hollering was about. He'd obviously gone to check on the bullocks and left the gate open, but luckily they had turned immediately left and were wandering down the track to Little Orchards. "Stupid man!" I thought. "I suppose I'd better go and help him round them up before they escape onto the lane and cause an accident." Will saw me coming and started shouting at me. "Come on Nipper, hurry up and get these cows back in their field. Go that way!" as he pointed his bony finger in the general direction of the bullocks. I completely took no notice of him and ran far out to the right so that I could bring the bullocks back along the track on the same side as the field they had just escaped from. If the Weasel had any sense, he would realise my plan and go and stand out in the lane and hold the gate open, but no, he started following me down the track.

Just as I managed to turn the bullocks and had them heading in the right direction, they saw the Weasel who was now waving his arms around and still shouting ridiculous instructions at me. This, of course, resulted in frightening the cows. They then turned sharply and started running flat out towards me. The trouble was they were heading into a dead end as the gate was shut at the bottom of the track. There was only one thing for it. I had to bark a warning to them to slow them down and let them know I was going to stand my ground – they could not come this way. Thank goodness, they seemed to understand me, but unfortunately I must have over done it. They did duly slow down, but when they saw the closed gate, they whipped round and were now galloping back towards the Weasel.

As I raced up behind them and started to overtake them, we all passed the Weasel who had spread-eagled himself on the fence. I soon realised I was not going to make it in front of them before they reached the lane. I had to think quickly about my next course of action. I needed to stay one step ahead of the bullocks. I shot under the fence on the left side of the track and cut the corner across the bean field and raced to the hedge along the top of the field and pushed my through the thorny branches and out onto the lane. Luckily for me, I had guessed which way the bullocks would turn. I walked forward towards them, zigzagging across the lane, making myself look as big as possible and then I barked. We were now face to face; 28 bullocks and little old me in a 'stand-off'.

What made him do it, I will never fathom, but the Weasel eventually arrived at the entrance to Little Orchards. He then came through the gate into the bean field and started walking towards me on the other side of the hedge. Unfortunately he didn't shut the gate behind him and it swung wide open. I now couldn't see him, but I heard him pass me, mumbling away to himself. The bullocks heard him too. You can imagine what happened next. The bullocks slowly turned and headed straight for the open gate; once through it, they took off and roared round, galloping this way and that, kicking up their heels. The Weasel let out an ear-piercing "Nipper!" It took seconds for the bullocks to trample their way through the beans. I guessed I was in real trouble with the Weasel now. I crept along the lane and stuck my nose round the gateway. Will saw me and growled at me "Get here now!" and pointed at his feet. Boy, he looked mad. I gingerly walked forward, keeping my head down. I didn't dare look at his face. He had also started to march in my direction, still mumbling and cursing. As he went to pass me, he turned and I just caught sight of him bring his leg back.

I let out a huge yelp as he kicked me in the ribs and bowled me over. I was completely winded, but I managed to drag myself a few feet away under the shade of the hedge and then just lay there, trying to catch my breath. I kept one eye on Will, who was heading for the gate and to my sheer relief Tom and Becky pulled up in the gateway. Tom jumped out of the car and was heading this way with a look of fury on his face. He marched up to Will, grabbed a handful of his shirt and tie and lifted the Weasel a foot of the ground with his left arm and in the same instant drew his right arm back with a clenched fist. Before he swung the punch, Becky ran up beside Tom and shouted at him "Tom, put him down". Tom let him down, but hung onto his shirt. He then growled in Will's face "How dare you – if you ever go near Nipper again, I will report you, trust me I will!"

Will had gone very pale and whimpered back "but that useless dog tried to kill me. He deliberately stampeded the cattle at me, let them out on the lane, then drove them into bean field and had them charging round, ruining the crop." As Tom let go of Will he replied "what nonsense, Nipper is a brilliant dog – you just don't understand him. It would be best if you just leave him alone and let me handle him." There was a pause before Tom said to Will "Right let's say no more about it and get these bullocks back where they are supposed to be. Can I suggest you man the gate".

Becky came and crouched down beside me and stroked my head. Her eyes were full of tears "I'm so sorry Nipper; are you alright?" I recovered quickly, but I was enjoying the attention. Becky told me to stay where I was and she'd go and get the car; she thought I should go to the vets and get checked over. I jumped up and wagged my tail – see I'm fine, really I am. There's absolutely no need for vets. "You old rogue" she said, "there's me worrying myself about you, but you're as tuff as old boots. Come on then let's get these bullocks back in their field and go and find Tina."

Chapter 9

Comings and Goings

I awoke to the very summer sound of the magpies carrying on. In fact, they were making quite a racket, tapping their beaks on the upstairs cottage windows, probably waking up Tom and Becky. They actually sound like their laughing and up to no good. My ribs were a little sore, but once I'd had a little stretch and starting moving about, I soon forget all about my aches. I felt a little anxious this morning but couldn't decide why that was. Perhaps it was having to face the Weasel or was there a storm coming? It was already very warm, in fact I would even say quite muggy.

Tom and Becky were soon up and sure enough, the magpies had woken them too. I heard Tom moaning about them to Tina as he opened the door and let her out. "Good morning Nipper, how are you today?" enquired Tom, but before I could answer, Tina and I were off, racing round the garden. "Well that answers that young man. You seem no worse for wear, thank goodness. Perhaps that's just as well; we'll have a busy morning loading up the bullocks and I could do with your help, but I promise you, I will be with you the whole time – you stick with me kid" said Tom.

Almost as soon as Becky drove off to work, the lorry turned up to collect the bullocks. Tom and I joined the Weasel across the road by the field gate. He looked a bit flustered, I thought. "The lorry has turned up early; we need to get these cows up to the farm and into the holding pen for loading, Tom." There was a slight pause and then he said "I'm sorry about yesterday. You had every right to hit me; I was well out of order. What would you like me to do?" said Will. "Well for starters, it's Nipper you need to apologise too, but I did say, we'd say no more about it. But please, don't let me catch you doing anything like that again. Right, how about you man the gates again and Nipper and I will go and fetch the beasts."

This was going to be tricky, I thought. Those bullocks have got wind of something; they were heading at a gallop, to the other side of the field. Perhaps the lorry has upset them. Tom and I set off in opposite directions and we soon had the bullocks back up at the gate where Will was waiting. He'd roped off the lane either side of the gate, so the bullocks could cross straight over the lane up into the farm yard. He opened the gate and I coaxed the bullocks forward by trotting from side to side behind them and occasionally nipping their heels. Once they were all out of the field, Tom closed the gate behind us; all was going well until they saw the lorry. The two bullocks at the front swung to the right and charged through the rope, which, surprise, surprise, wasn't tied securely enough for their weight. It took seconds for them to reach Tom's garden; they managed to squeeze themselves between the smallest gap at the end of the fence and the hedge. The rest, of course, followed. They were up the bank and running round the lawn and trampling on Becky's lovely flowers.

Tom shouted to Will "Change of plan. You run up to the farm and open the top gate to the garden and I'll push them through that way". With that Will ran off up the farm track and Tom and I made sure we kept them going forward. Thank goodness that worked; we soon had them in the loading pen and shortly after that, they were all loaded and heading off in the lorry.

Tom invited Will down to the cottage for a cup of tea and some breakfast. He said to Will "I don't know what spooked the cows this morning, but I feel a storm coming and the midges are already very irritating." Will agreed with him. Tom carried onto say "I don't think Becky will be too pleased when she sees her gladioli later; or rather the lack of them. She really hates it when the animals go off. She was a bit upset this morning when she went to work. I told her the bullocks were going to market; I did not tell her they were going to the slaughterhouse and I'd appreciate it, if you didn't let on either. She'll be sad enough when she sees all her hard work out there is ruined.

Tom was right. He, Tina and I were waiting in the front garden when Becky came home. Tom walked over to meet her and started to apologise and explain what had happened. Poor Becky, she really did look upset, the tears were running down her face. Tom put his arm round Becky and Tina and I sat down either side of her and leant on her legs. Tom handed Becky his handkerchief and once she'd wiped her tears away, she croaked out "I couldn't care less about the flowers. It's the 28 cow pats that are left on the lawn to remind me they've gone". Tom started to laugh; "you are the funniest lady I've ever met. You never cease to amaze me with your logic. Come on inside and I'll make us a cup of tea. I've got the rest of the day off, so I'll clear up the mess". He kissed her on the forehead and in they went.

After tea, Becky and Tina headed off down to the horses and invited me to go with them. I was pleased to see, she seemed a little happier now. The horses were all swishing their tails and there was a lot of head nodding and foot stamping going on when we arrived. "Oh you poor things" said Becky. "I won't be a minute; I'll soon have you sorted out with some fly spray". She started with Lady, who was obviously well used to being sprayed all over. Becky squirted some on a cloth and wiped it all round Lady's face. It was amazing, all the flies, except for a stubborn few just disappeared. Next she covered Chicory, then Toby, but when she reached Wills she gasped "Oh mate, you're in a mess, I think we need to get you into a stable away from these midges. You're being eaten alive and you've rubbed yourself raw". With that she led Wills round to the stables and sorted out some hay and buckets of water for him. Becky put some sort of potion on Wills neck and at the top of this tail and told him she'd be back later, after dark, to let him out.

We then headed back up to the cottage and once we were out of sight, Becky stopped to listen and made sure Wills remained quiet. She said to Tina and me "I just want to listen for a minute. I don't want poor Wills to worry about being left in on his own; but I think he is more than happy to be in and away from those midges – they're driving me nuts today – I can always put Chicory in with him for company if needs be." Once Becky was satisfied Wills was going to be alright, we headed home for our tea.

There was definitely a storm brewing; the air was thick and clammy. I felt very lethargic tonight, but also a little tense with worry about the impending thunder and lightning. Tom and Becky stayed indoors for the evening, probably because of the midges, but I missed their company out in the garden. I retired early to my armchair as the first rumble began in the distance.

It was about midnight when an almighty crash of thunder was right overhead. It had already started raining and I was shaking with fear. The back door of the cottage suddenly opened and out rushed Becky. She was wearing pyjamas, cagoule and wellington boots and clutching the car keys. "Nipper! I've completely forgotten to let Wills out. He'll be so fed up with me. Do you want to come for a ride?" I was glad of the distraction and as Becky opened the car door, I jumped up onto the driver's seat and bounced across; well more like pushed across to the passenger seat, as Becky leapt in behind me.

We roared off down to Little Orchards, where Becky jumped out and ran across the yard to the stables. "I'm really sorry Wills, come on, out you come. At least the midges will have gone for now" she said as she slung a rope over Wills head and lead him round to the field. I followed and by the time Becky had closed the field gate and we'd run back to the car, we were soaked.

When we got back to the cottage, Becky invited me in again "come on boy, you need towelling down and you don't want to be out here on your own do you." So I stepped into the kitchen and had a good nose round. Becky fetched a towel and returned to the kitchen and started drying me off. Tina obviously heard Becky talking to me and trotted down the stairs to see what was going on. "What are you doing in here?" she asked as she sidled up to me. "Well I was invited in; I hope you don't mind, I'll just sit by the back door if that's alright with you" I replied. "Yes, of course, that's fine, but you better stay in the kitchen. Only I'm allowed upstairs" said Tina. I guess she was a little nervous that I was treading on her territory, but I understood this was her house and she was a little prone to jealousy, as far as Tom and Becky were concerned.

Becky left the back door open for me and said goodnight. About every half an hour for the rest of the night Tina, trotted down to see me and make sure I had stayed in the kitchen. I was actually curled up on the back door mat and pretended to be asleep, but I heard her come down the stairs and a couple of times felt her nudge my back. I don't know why, but I didn't feel scared of the storm anymore. Just being in with Tom and Becky and Tina was comforting, even though I could see my armchair just six feet away.

Chapter 10

Tina Gets in A Pickle

Becky had a week's holiday from work and had planned all manner of things. Tom and the Weasel were busy combining and getting the straw in from the field ready for winter. It was going to be a good week. It was glorious weather and best of all; I had Tina and Becky's company all day.

Becky and Monica had arranged to go for a ride round the farm, so Tina and I joined them. We had to be called several times to catch up. Rabbit and fox scents can be jolly distracting. Becky didn't seem to understand that we always kept an eye on where she was and that we could look after ourselves. To be fair though, whenever Becky called us, we also enjoyed the race back to her. Tina just had the edge over me and would delight in telling me "I was first, I was first". It was all said in good humour though.

We all galloped up to the gate by the big beech tree and Becky jumped off Lady to open it. She was struggling with the padlock with one hand and holding Lady with the other. Lady was really excited after her gallop and was busting to get going again. Becky told her to stand still for a minute and let go of the reins so she could sort the padlock out. As the gate opened, Becky went to grab Lady's reins, but she tripped on a bit of rough ground and before you could blink, Lady was through the gate and galloping off up the track while we all stood and watched, open mouthed. Califfe then started to dance around and whinny; he obviously wanted to race after Lady. I could sense Mon and Becky were worried. I thought I better do something, before things got of control. I told Tina to stay where she was, as I raced off after Lady. Luckily Becky stayed with Califfe and Mon and started to call Lady back to her.

Boy! That Lady was quick on her little legs; I was never going to keep up with her. This was going to take some cunning. Once she reached the next gate, she slowed to a canter and did a large circle. She then dropped down to a high knee trot, completely showing off and so I managed to catch up a bit. Just as I reached the top of the hill, Lady heard Becky and Califfe calling and took off again at a flat out gallop back down the hill and straight back to Becky. Typical! I thought, as I quickly turned and chased her back down the hill.

Becky held her arms up high "whoa, whoa girl". She grabbed the reins and patted her neck. "You rascal, you've upset Califfe. You know we are supposed to go riding together, you cheeky monkey". With that Becky quickly vaulted on and found her stirrups. "Everyone alright?" she said as she looked at Mon. "Sorry about that, my fault." She then looked at me, as I returned panting and said "Thanks' Nipper, I thought I had a long walk home for a minute. You're a star". I wagged my tail in appreciation, but I didn't tell her it was nothing to do with me; Lady came back of her own accord.

We then took off again at a break-neck speed back to the top of the farm, Tina and myself bringing up the rear. I was going to sleep well tonight! At least now it was nearly all downhill on the way home. The ride home was in fact quite leisurely. We ambled along the field track and deviated through the woods, which Tina and I really enjoyed, as we could again investigate all the haunts of the deer and foxes. They then rode back out into the fields again, with Becky and Mon chatting away all the time. This was just so much fun, with the girls distracted; Tina and I could do some more exploring.

Once home, the horses washed and groomed off and returned to their fields, Mon came round for a coffee and more chatting. Those two could talk for England and their favourite subject; in fact their only subject was, of course, horses. I overheard Becky telling Mon that Lady's official registered name was 'Lady Harvest Gold', but Becky had an unofficial name for her which was 'Lady Flamingo'. Mainly because she was so graceful, but more because she didn't half 'Flamin-go'! Both ladies were laughing at this and Mon agreed she was very quick on her feet and even a bit head strong. Becky went on to explain that Lady had been used as a racing pony in her younger days and still felt she had to race everywhere. Lady had given the previous owners a few scares and sadly they made the decision to have Lady put down. They were worried she was going to cause a serious accident, but after much persuasion, agreed to hand her over to Becky as she was over 18 and seemed to get on so well with her.

Eventually Mon went home and Becky started banging around in the kitchen. I have no idea what she was up to, but there was soon a very sweet, almost sickly smell wafting out through the door.

A couple of hours later Becky came out into the garden with a cheese sandwich and a cup of tea and sat at the table. She was looking at a book for some time, while she slowly ate her lunch. Tina and I had to be patient for our sandwich corners today. I think I must have nodded off, because I was unaware that Tina had gone back into the house until I heard a shriek from Becky. "How could you Tina! You bad girl! It took me ages to make that Tomato Chutney and you've ruined it. I can't believe you've licked the top off every jar – you deserve to be sick. I suggest you keep out of my way until I've calmed down". With that Becky stomped out into the garden and went over to the flower bed and started weeding. Tina lay down by the back door with her head on her paws, looking a bit sheepish.

I've never heard Becky shout at Tina before, although there have been plenty of occasions when Tina has been naughty, especially stealing food. I decided to keep my head down and out of the way, so I crept off up to the farm.

I went and found Tom and followed him around for the rest of the afternoon. I thought it best to wait until Tom finished work and return to the cottage with him. I'm glad I did. As soon as we walked down the garden path and he called "hello" to Becky, it was obvious she was still not happy. "What's the matter?" asked Tom. "Oh, I made a load of Tomato Chutney this morning. It's my fault, I left the jars on top of the fridge to cool down with a cover on them and Tina decided to try it. She ate the top out of every single jar, so I had to throw the whole lot away. I feel really bad about it now, as I told her off and said she deserved to be sick. Guess what? She was. I've spent the afternoon clearing up after her and scrubbing the new landing carpet. I think she's feeling a bit sorry for herself; as am I. I just can't believe a dog would want to eat tomato chutney, but I should have known Tina will eat anything". Tom put his arm round Becky and gave her a kiss. "Never mind love; I'm sure it would have been delicious. We can always get some more tomatoes if you want to have another go" said Tom. "Maybe in a few days; I've gone off the idea just now" replied Becky.

Becky walked over to Tina who had come to sit next to me. She crouched down next to her and gave her a hug and rubbed her chest and behind her ears and she then did the same to me. "Poor old Tina" said Becky, "not one of our better days. I hope you'll forgive me. How about a bowl of porridge? That should settle your tummy". With that, Becky went in and made both Tina and I an unexpected bowl of porridge in the afternoon. Tina admitted to me later; the chutney wasn't very nice, she didn't know why she'd eaten it – it was just there." I don't think she'll do that again, especially after being so sick.

The following morning, after our walk, Becky took Tina off in the car. I have to say, I was disappointed; even fed up. I had hoped to spend the day with them, just lazing around in the warm sunshine. Lazing around can be quite boring when you've no-one to talk to or even just have their company. You can imagine I was pleasantly surprised when they returned within the hour. Not only that, Becky had brought her friend Avril home with her.

This was the first time I'd met Avril. She was a very 'bubbly' and friendly lady and seemed pleased to meet me and the feeling was most definitely mutual. Becky told her to make herself comfortable out in the garden while she made some tea. I wondered why she'd put the deckchairs out there before she left. Unfortunately, Avril had German Measles and wasn't allowed to go to work, so although she was off sick; she didn't feel sick at all.

After they'd had their tea and delicious sticky buns, which they shared with Tina and I; the girls started chatting and laughing; absolutely non-stop all morning. It transpired that Becky and Avril had known each other for a while and had become good friends. I overheard that Tom and Becky had taken Richard to the local pub with them last Friday evening, where he met Avril. It was fairly evident from listening to the girls chatting that Avril was rather taken with Richard and it would appear visa-versa. Becky was saying how lovely it would be if Richard and Avril were to marry and live in the cottage next door or one of the other cottages on the farm. Avril told Becky "hang on, not so fast, we've only just met and you're marrying us off already; you old match-maker".

All in all, it turned out to be a very pleasant and relaxed day; even though Tina and I didn't get to snooze much with all the giggling and chatter.

It's true what they say; 'there is never a dull moment on a farm'. Since Tom and Becky moved into the cottage and in particular, Tina, I can confirm this statement to be true. Shortly after the tomato chutney incident, there were two catastrophes at the same time.

Becky had been slaving away in the kitchen, making some homemade tomato soup for lunch. Tom came down from the farm for an early lunch; he must have smelt it cooking. "That smell's good" he told Becky. "I'm starving". Just as Becky was about to dish it up, there was an almighty crash at the front of the cottage. I didn't have to bark this time; we all heard it. Tom and Becky rushed out to the front to find two cars with huge dents in each of the bonnets. Both drivers were out of their cars and blaming each other for driving too fast round the bend. Tom chatted to them for some time and eventually they agreed it was six of one and half a dozen of the other and yes, perhaps they were going a bit too fast for a narrow windy country lane. Both cars were still driveable and after exchanging addresses; they drove off.

Becky was first back through the kitchen door and let out an ear-piercing shriek "Tina!" Tom ran in to see what had happened and as I stuck my nose through the door, it looked like a blood bath. On seeing red splashed all over the walls and ceiling, Becky naturally assumed that Tina had cut herself badly and had crawled off to die somewhere. Actually, on closer inspection, it was, of course, the tomato soup. Tom decided that as there was none on the floor, Tina had already cleaned up the evidence and when she heard Becky coming, went to hide in the hallway. Tom further concluded that Tina must have jumped up at the cooker, landed on the ladle that had been left in the saucepan. This in turn tossed the saucepan lid in the air and flicked the soup in two different directions with some force and then, amazingly, the lid came back down on the saucepan, the right way up.

After lunch, I asked Tina if she was still in trouble, but she just shrugged "No, of course, not. They love me and everything I do. Initially, they were so worried I'd hurt myself, they forgot I'd been naughty! But in their eyes, I never am. They always blame themselves for putting temptation in my way". With that she ran off round the garden, wagging her tail and wanting to play.

Chapter 11

The Kids Come to Stay

At the end of the week, Tom's sister, Lesley and his niece and nephew, Elaine and Alan, turned up to go riding. When they arrived, Becky suggested they spent a little time in the garden playing ball with Tina, so that she got used to them. Becky whispered to Lesley "I just wanted to make sure Tina was happy in their company because of her past history with children". From what I saw, Elaine and Alan and Tina all got on like a 'house on fire'. They were certainly great fun as far as I was concerned. We all played together while Lesley and Becky had a chat and some coffee.

"Right kids" said Becky, "Let's go riding. We'll walk down to Little Orchards". The kids were obviously excited and ran on ahead with Tina and I, as Becky and Lesley strolled down the track. It was another hot day, but at least there was a pleasant summer breeze.

Lady was fetched from the field and the kids helped Becky brush her coat and her beautiful flaxen mane and tail. She looked lovely and was certainly enjoying all the attention and the mints. Just as Becky went into the tack room to fetch the saddle, I heard it. I trotted round to the other side of the yard and headed up the track and stopped and listened. There it was again; a faint, but frantic mooing. I moved forward again, ears pricked. The noise was coming from the far side of the field on my right. I wriggled through the hedge and cantered across the field towards the woods.

As I came closer, it didn't take long to figure out what the problem was. I slowed right down to a walk, so I didn't upset the cow further; she was obviously very upset. She was one of the cows that had recently had a calf and was standing precariously at the top of the bank trying to encourage her calf to climb out of the ditch. This wasn't going to be easy. There was an old dried up stream at the bottom of the bank which was a good six feet down. The main trouble was the trees that were very overgrown with thick tree roots criss-crossing over the ditch. The poor calf was in a real fix. He'd ducked under some of the roots and climbed over others and now couldn't move forwards or backwards. I needed help. I ran back towards Little Orchards, barking as I went.

Becky meanwhile had finished tacking up and was leading Elaine, proudly sitting on Lady out to the field. Luckily for me though, it didn't take Becky long to work out something was wrong. As I arrived, Becky turned to me "Nipper, what's wrong?" I barked again. "Okay, Nipper, we're on our way. You'll need to show us what's up." Becky had already turned Lady round and was heading back to the stables. She explained to the kids "sorry guys, something's wrong. When Nipper barks, something is most definitely going on. We'll have to put Lady back in the field and ride another day. We really need to hurry up and see what's bothering Nipper".

Unfortunately they couldn't squeeze through the hedge, so had to run up the track to the gate, but they were soon heading in my direction and could see the cow at the top of the bank. By now the cow was making quite a racket, the pitch had gone up several notches and she was now almost hysterical. She was very worried about her baby. I watched Becky and the others come towards me and barked at them to hurry up.

As they arrived, Becky realised very quickly she would need Tom's help; but where was he? She asked Lesley and the kids to stay with the cow and calf, but not too close and she would run up to the farm to find Tom. Before she was half way across the field, we saw Tom heading down the drive towards us; he had obviously heard me barking and heard the racket the cow was making. As Becky neared Tom, she shouted to him that the calf was stuck in the ditch and he would need a chainsaw and some rope. Tom turned tail and went to fetch the necessary and Becky returned to the bank.

It wasn't long before Tom turned up in the Landrover and gathered the chainsaw and rope from the back. "Hi kids" he said, "what's going on here then? Oh, I see. How on earth did this little fellow get in such a jam? We'll soon have him out." Tom clambered down the bank to the calf and made up a halter which he put round the calf's nose and up over his head. He then gently pulled the calf's nose round and away from the tree root, so it was facing its tail. To Becky he said "I'm going to have to start up the chainsaw; do you think you can hold the calf still so I can cut away those roots. This is going to be very scary for him, but I'll be as quick and as careful as I can. If he moves, the chainsaw is going to be very close to your arm – do you trust me?" Becky looked a little worried, but was quick to answer "of course I trust you; I can't see any other way of getting him out."

Becky glanced at Elaine, Alan and Lesley, who all looked on with worried faces. "It will be fine kids, don't worry; the little fellow will be out of here in a jiffy" she told them. Tom started up the chainsaw at the top of the bank and carefully climbed down. "Are you alright Becky? Ready to begin? Hang on tight to his head" said Tom. Tom started to cut the root on the far side of the ditch. The saw sliced threw it like butter. I was relieved to see the calf didn't budge; which was pretty amazing as the saw was very loud and spitting sawdust all over him and Becky. He seemed to accept that Tom and Becky were trying to help him. He was probably a bit tired after struggling to get out on his own for a while.

Tom moved onto the next root that was lying underneath the calf and then the next. He'd cut away all the roots on the far side and had now repositioned himself in front of Becky and the calf so he could keep an eye on them; as well as where he was cutting. He left the final root that was above him until last. I presume he did that to keep the calf immobilised until he'd finished. As he turned off the saw and laid it down on the bank, he pulled all the roots out of the way. He said to Becky "well done you; I've never been so nervous in all my life. The chain missed your arm by inches. I was really scared the calf was going to move. We'll swap places now; I don't want you hurt as he breaks for freedom". They quickly swapped places and Tom let the calf's head turn forward. "Come on you, you lucky boy; I'll lead the way, you follow". With that Tom slowly scrambled up the bank leading the calf, but the little chap seemed a bit reluctant. Tom turned and gathered the calf up, front and back, in his strong arms and gently lifted the calf up. Once he started to move him, the calf thrashed out with his legs, suddenly realising he was free. Tom just managed to face him in the right direction up the bank and pushed him forward, as the calf leapt for freedom.

He made the cutest little noise as soon as his legs hit the grass and started cavorting about. His mum then let out a loud 'moo', as if to tell him off. He rushed over to her and soon had his head buried under her tummy and started to suckle some milk. Everyone started laughing, as his little tail was wagging so fast. The kids asked if they could name him 'Lucky'. Tom said "Clumsy would be more appropriate", but after the groans from Elaine and Alan, he had to agree 'Lucky' was okay.

As they made their way back to the cottage, Becky said "I'm sorry about the riding, but I think you'll agree that was more exciting. We'll go riding again at the weekend when you come to stay. Anyway, I've had an idea. How about we go and fetch Sheena and head up to The Downs for a walk and an ice-cream. How does that sound?" They all thought that was a great idea. The kids jumped in the car and before we were invited, Tina and I leapt in the back and off we went. "Who's Sheena?" I asked Tina. "Oh, she belongs to them. She's a lively liver and white spaniel. She's good company on walks, but I really don't like her coming into my house and I've told her so a few times too. Trouble is; I then get told off by Tom and Becky for being grumpy."

I'd never been to The Downs before; I was intrigued. It took about half an hour in the car and when we arrived, there were several other cars already parked; we just managed to squeeze into the last parking space. The kids jumped out of the car with Sheena, who had been on the back seat with them and Becky came to open the hatchback for Tina and I. "Stay close you lot, until we're over the style and away from the road. We'll have to go this way today as there's sheep on the other-side" said Becky. So we duly walked to heal until we were through the first gate. I stuck close to Tina and Sheena, as I didn't know where I was, but there were some wonderful smells and I was itching to investigate them.

Tina was right, Sheena was good fun to be with and the three of us raced around, sniffing here and there and often ran back to Becky and the others. This was an amazing place. The views were spectacular, we were really high up and the breeze was throwing all sorts of wonderful smells at us. We walked for about an hour and then turned round to walk back to the car. Becky suggested to Lesley that they go and fetch the ice-cream while the kids stayed with us dogs and found somewhere to sit. They returned a little while later armed with seven white things balanced on cones. They handed the kids theirs and Becky asked Elaine to hold one for Tina, while she held one for me and Lesley had Sheena's. Tina started licking the ice-cream and had bolted hers down in seconds, as had Sheena. I was a bit apprehensive, but it didn't take me long to get the hang of it. I soon realised you had to eat it quickly or bits melted and fell to the floor; where, of course, Tina was waiting.

People passed by us laughing; saying things like "how cute" and "I suppose we better get one for our dog". As we returned to the car; the man in the ice-cream van shouted across to us; holding up his thumb "thanks for that. Trade has just doubled".

We returned home, having had a wonderful afternoon. I don't know who was more exhausted; the kids or us dogs, but I really hope I will be taken up to the Downs again; I really did enjoy my ice-cream.

Two days later, the kids were back. Lesley and their Dad, Paul, dropped them off with overnight bags. Apparently they were coming to stay with Tom and Becky for the Bank Holiday weekend, while Paul and Lesley went on a short break to Jersey.

The weekend flew by. Becky had arranged every minute of the two days with riding Lady, long walks with Tina and myself. We also had great fun down at Little Orchards collecting apples for the kids to make apple pies. Tina kept getting told off for eating the apples they dropped. I couldn't understand her love for them; they were so sharp in taste – not for me thank you. There was then lots of laughter from the kitchen while they made the pies. From what I could see through the open door, the kids were covered in white stuff and so was the floor.

Chapter 12

Lambing Time

The huge barn was the same size as the local football pitch. It was stacked with straw from floor to ceiling; winter was well on its way. The combine harvester had been cleaned off and serviced ready for next year. It was parked up in the centre, at the front of barn, along with the two big red tractors. To the left of the entrance was a small office and behind that was a small area, where all the tools and spare parts were kept and behind that was a massive pen for the cows. It ran for over 100ft and was about 30ft wide with a cattle trough running the full length along the front. This was in two parts; at the base was the actual trough where the cows were fed hard food and the manger ran above it for the hay. Tom and Will skilfully delivered the hay or silage with the bucket on front of the tractor. On the other side of the barn as you entered, immediately to the right was a large silo full of corn. Just behind that the most enormous bags of fertiliser which were stacked one on top of the other, all the way up to the roof. Then there was a huge stack of straw for winter bedding.

I had helped gather in all the sheep yesterday; which had been separated into two large pens. The one along the back wall held the older sheep, who'd all lambed before. The other pen at the back on the right hand side was for the sheep who were about to have their first set of lambs.

Also down the middle of the barn were smaller man-made pens, where each new Mum and her lambs were moved; once they were born. These were made out of small straw bales stacked up three high and on three sides, with gate hurdlers at the front. Above each one was a heat lamp hanging down from the rafters and plenty of straw bedding underneath to keep the new arrivals warm.

The vet had been today to check the sheep and predicted that it wouldn't be long before the first lambs started appearing. He'd thought at least half a dozen sheep might even start lambing within the next couple of days. From now on, each night, either Tom or Becky would come up and check the sheep before they turned in for the night and then again one or t'other of them would come out just after midnight. I was always pleased to see them and accept a pat on the head or a chest rub. "All okay Nipper?" they'd ask me. They didn't talk much in the early hours. They just shone their torch round, checked all the sheep for any signs of impending birth and went back to bed.

When the sheep were in and it was lambing time, I always stayed up in the barn with them. In fact it was luxury sleeping in the straw. I think the sheep were happy to have me around to look after them, especially when they started lambing. Foxes were often prowling around for a quick and easy meal, so I had to keep my wits about me.

Becky was getting impatient for the lambs to arrive. Apparently she'd been on a lambing course at the local agricultural college in Plumpton and was busting to try her hand. The following evening she came up to the barn early in the evening. She was well dressed for the cold, with woolly hat and gloves and one of Tom's thick coats on over her own. She came and found me and asked if she could join me for a while. As you can imagine, I was more than pleased for the company. She walked over to the sheep and had a good look round, then grabbed a straw bale and brought it over to where I'd been lying and sat down. She'd brought a book with her and, although the lights were on in the barn, she had also brought a torch to read by.

About every fifteen minutes she put her book down and walked over to the sheep; shone the torch round, then went and sat down again. This went on for a couple of hours until Tom arrived. "Come on Becky, bedtime. Have you never heard 'a watched pot never boils'" said Tom. He wandered over to check the sheep and then said "goodnight" to me. To be honest, I was quite pleased Becky had gone down to the house. At least now I could get some sleep. All this up and down every few minutes was beginning to get tiresome.

The following two nights were the same; Becky arriving shortly after 7 o'clock; staying for a couple of hours, but still no lambs. Lambs are quite often born at night time, but, of course, the first one came during the morning when Becky was at work. In fact, it was a healthy set of twins and Tom was on hand to make sure the birth went smoothly. I could see when Becky was told on her return from work, she was disappointed she missed it, but there were still 200 sheep to lamb, so I felt sure she'd help with some of them.

Typically, once one starts, they all start and, of course, that night Becky got her chance to help. As soon as she arrived up at the barn after her dinner, she shone her torch round and 2 sheep had signs of lambs coming. She ran off down to the house to get Tom and was back in a minute. Tom quickly followed and told Becky to wait and watch. "Let's just see if the sheep can cope on their own first, before we go rushing in" said Tom. "Alright! Alright!" Becky whispered back a bit impatiently. "It's just I'm so excited". "Oh I hadn't noticed!" said Tom "and why are you whispering?" "I don't want to disturb the expectant Mums; they need to have a calm and relaxed environment" she whispered again. Tom shook his head slowly and smiled.

A little while later, Tom climbed in with the sheep and invited Becky to help him. "Come on then, I think this one in the corner needs a hand. Tom took hold of the tiny feet that were just visible; one in each hand. Talking all the time to the expectant Mum; he gently pulled the feet towards himself and within seconds, out popped a soggy wet lamb. Tom wiped all the mucus and birth sack away from the little'uns face and stood back; he could see it was breathing, so he let nature take its course. Mum slowly got up; started nuzzling her new baby, licking it clean and nudging it to stand up. Within minutes the lamb was standing and Mum soon had it cleaned off; it actually looked like a lamb now. The little fellow started bleating for food. His instinct took over and he began head butting Mum in the sides several times, before he found what he was looking for underneath – some milk.

Tom said to Becky "I'm fairly sure this old girl will be having another one shortly; so we'll keep an eye on her. Do you fancy making us some coffee; I think we are in for a long night; I've been watching those two over there and they look like they're just starting".

Becky made the coffee in double quick time and was back in what seemed like minutes, armed with a flask and a couple of mugs. While she was gone, Tom and I ushered the new Mum and her lambs into one of the small home-made pens and when Becky returned and stood to see what Tom was looking at; she now saw there were two little lambs. "That was quick" said Becky. "She managed the second one on her own while I was checking the others" replied Tom. "They seem to have got hang of the milk bar, so we'll go and sort out the others."

Sure enough, two more sheep had started, so Tom suggested he take one and Becky the other. Becky took her coat off even though it was so cold; rolled up her sleeves and knelt down in the straw. Like Tom, she gently eased the lamb out. She was really pleased it had all gone smoothly; she really didn't want to ask for Tom's help on this one. Almost as soon as her bundle landed on the straw, she could see another pair of feet sticking out of Mum. She quickly checked the first lamb's nostrils and mouth were clear and as she turned back, a second lamb was half way out; so she helped it on its way.

Tom, Becky and I moved all the new arrivals, fifteen in all, to their new pens and made sure they were settled. They eventually went off to bed around 2am with an instruction to me to bark if I needed them. I was chuffed to bits they trusted my judgement, but I hoped the rest of the night would be quiet so we could all get some sleep.

All in all, it was just over three weeks before all the lambs were born to the older sheep. They had done really well and produced several pairs of twins and even a few triplets. Tom and Will managed to persuade some of the older sheep with single lambs to take on one or two of the triplets, but there were still eleven lambs that needed bottle feeding for one reason or another. Some of the sheep weren't such good mothers and would not let the lambs suckle. The bottle lambs were all placed in a pen on their own and

Becky was in her element feeding them whenever she could. They all had a big blue 'B' for bottle sprayed on their backs and Becky started calling them Bobby, Brian, Bertie, Baxter and so on; I lost count of all their names and I think really, so did she.

Chapter 13

The Combine Harvester Fire

I can't believe Tom and Becky have been here for over a year. It is a very hot day; the hottest day of the year so far and it is Tom's birthday today. He and Will are in the field opposite the cottage and are combining the barley field. The weather has been dry for weeks and the dust from the combine's huge wheels is blowing across the field in the strong westerly breeze. I thought I'd sit up here on the Tom's front lawn for two reasons and watch proceedings. Firstly, I'm in the shade and secondly, away from the dust squalls. Also, Becky will be home soon, which means I'll have Tina for company and quite likely, Becky will take the men some tea and cake when she gets home. Just as the thought entered my head, I could hear Becky's car coming down the lane and I could also hear Tina starting to squeak inside the cottage in anticipation of Becky's arrival.

While Becky made the tea for the men, Tina and I had a romp round the garden and I told her about my boring day lying around waiting for her to come out and play. She responded with "you've had a boring day! I've been stuck in the house, looking at four walls; it's also very noisy in there today with the combine droning on, up and down the field; I've hardly had a wink of sleep". "Oh well, we're both out now. Let's see if we can't get ourselves some cake; that will cheer you up" I replied. But Tina was way ahead of me, she scuttled over the road and was hot on Becky's heals.

Will pulled the combine up at the hedge and turned off the engine and Tom followed suit in the baler, while Becky walked towards them with mugs of tea and cake. Not just ordinary cake, this was a huge chocolate Birthday cake for Tom. Tina and I sat down and waited patiently for any leftovers. While the three of them chatted, we watched every mouthful.

As the dust settled, I could smell something odd. I know it's a hot day, but I could definitely smell something familiar, but not right. What was it? I lifted my nose and sniffed and sniffed. There it was again – a bonfire perhaps? That's sort of what it smelt like, but there's no smoke anywhere and who on earth would have a bonfire on a day like this.

I looked up at Becky to see if any cake was coming my way, but I was distracted by the smell. There it was again, quite strong now. It wafted across in front of me. I sniffed again and then I saw the flames, only small ones, but the combine harvester was most definitely on fire. I jumped up and barked. I could feel all eyes were on me. Tom was quick to ask me "what is it Nipper?", as we exchanged glances. He soon worked out what I was looking at. "Oh! The combines on fire" he said as he rushed over to it, followed by Will. He climbed up the steps, two at a time and pulled himself up on the hand rail with one arm, as he was still clutching his mug of tea in the other. He threw the tea at the flames and they were gone. "That was close" he said to Will, who had climbed up behind him. "I think the little bit of oil leakage has self-ignited in the heat" said Tom.

As they stood there looking at the spot, it suddenly ignited itself again. Will grabbed a rag and tried to dab out the flames, but to no avail. As fast as they were putting the flames out, more were jumping into life. "I think it's time to call the fire brigade said Will". He shouted at Becky to run to the house and call the Fire Brigade. She was off across the lane and up the drive. Luckily she'd left the back door open, so it didn't take long to ring for help and sure enough two fire engines arrived within ten minutes; both with sirens blaring and lights flashing.

Within a couple of minutes one fireman had doused the flames with foam, while another seven looked on. "Good job you called us out" he said. "You may think we've over reacted, but considering how dry the ground is, this could very quickly have turned into a disaster. You could have lost the combine and your field of straw in this breeze. Better to be safe rather than sorry."

The fire crews stayed for a while to keep a check on the combine. Actually, I think they all stayed so they could have a cup of tea and some cake, which Becky was pleased to provide. Tina and I did very well for cake corners that afternoon; not to mention all the fuss that was made of us.

Chapter 14

The Operation!

Next morning, I was up early and headed off again to see my girlfriend, Jess, down the main road. Unfortunately, Becky was up early and noticed I was missing. As I bounded up to Jess, some 20 minutes later; Becky was there to greet me. "And what exactly do you think you're up to young man" she asked? "Come on, jump up in the back" she said, as she held the door open for me. "I saw you heading off up the lane, you rascal. I guessed you were heading this way".

We returned home and went for our morning walk, and then Becky went off to work as usual. Once she was gone and Tom had left for the farm; I thought I'd try my luck again. I had a good look round and couldn't see anyone, so I legged it up the lane, making sure I kept near the hedge. The main road was really busy, a constant stream of cars, but no-one seem to notice me. I darted across the road and kept running down the hill to the spot in the hedge where I could duck under into the field. I was safe now; so continued at a steady jog. As I arrived at the kennels, their doors were open and Jess and the others were nowhere to be seen. I sniffed the air and followed her scent which took me round the back of the farm buildings. The farmer and one of the dogs were working with the sheep. Jess was lying down at the side of the field watching the proceedings. I crept along the edge of the field to join her. Unfortunately, the farmer saw me and came over and before I knew it, I was tied up and sitting in the back of his Landrover.

This really was getting tiresome, I thought. I just want to spend some time with Jess. Is that too much to ask? These humans just don't understand.

I was left there for over an hour before Tom came to fetch me. Well, at least it was Tom and not the Weasel. Tom didn't seem too pleased though and I was tied up once again when we got back to the farm. He did rub my head and apologised for tying me up, but I could just tell he was a bit fed up with me. "This can't go on Nipper. You really are becoming a nuisance in that department and you run the risk of being run over or shot by the farmer and we don't want that, do we?"

Both Tom and Becky were watching my every move for the rest of the day. Worse was to come though, I couldn't believe it – they shut the garage door on me, when they said goodnight. "Sorry Nipper, it's for your own good. The window's open a bit, but we just can't chance you running off again." Gosh, I was fed up!

The urge to go and see Jess was so great; her enticing smells were just too much to bear. I started looking for ways to escape. I climbed up on the chair, but Becky was right, I couldn't fit through the open window, try as I might. I prowled around the garage. I wondered if I could push the big garage door open. I wedged my body against it and shoved as hard as I could with my shoulder. It seemed to budge just a bit; I could just see light coming in underneath. I shoved again, and again it moved. I was really ramming my body against it now and eventually I had opened it enough to scramble out, but in my anxiousness to escape, I hadn't noticed how much noise I was making.

Just as I was about to make my bid for freedom, Becky was there; standing right in front of me. "Nipper – it's 4am and you've woken us up!" She raised her voice "Stop right there". She closed the door behind me and turned the handle tight. She led me back round to the side door and pointed for me to go in and on my armchair "just you get in there and be quiet. I know you want to go, but I'm sorry mate, you have to stay here". She crouched down and gave me a hug. "I'm really sorry Nipper, but I'm afraid it's a trip to the vets for you. This can't go on".

What does she mean? A trip to the vets? I'm not ill. The following morning I was to find out. After our walk, Becky forgot to put out my bowl of porridge, but instead asked me to jump into the car and sure enough we headed off to the vets. She stayed with me while they shaved off some of my coat on my paw. They then stuck a huge needle in while Becky tried to distract me by rubbing my ears and talking gently to me. The next thing I remember was trying to get up. What's wrong with me? Where am I and where's

Becky gone? I felt lousy and I whimpered. A young girl came over and opened the cage door I was in and stroked my head. "There's a good boy, it's alright" she said. "Your Mum will be here soon to collect you".

Sure enough 'Mum', Becky turned up to take me home. I felt really woozy and my legs would not walk me in a straight line to the door. I knew where I had come in and I knew I wanted to get out of here. When we reached home, Becky helped me out of the car and led me into the kitchen, where Tina greeted me with a lick of my face and plenty of nudges. "What's up with you Nipper? You don't smell very nice and you certainly don't look yourself, but I am really pleased to see you. I wondered where you were" she chirped. "Apparently, I've been castrated, whatever that means. I definitely don't want it done again. I'm sore, tired, hungry and fed up" I replied.

Becky led me to a large folded duvet on the other side of the kitchen. "You park yourself here Nipper and I'll get you something to eat" she said. I hadn't realised how hungry I was until she mentioned food and then I noticed a delicious smell as Becky was cutting up some meat in a bowl. "There you go you two, chicken and rice; just what the doctor or should I say vet, ordered". Tina and I ate side by side today and although she finished first, she left me to finish mine in peace. I sat back down on my duvet, curled up and went sound to sleep.

The next morning, I felt a lot better and after a short walk, enjoyed the chicken and rice again. In fact, Tina and I had that on the menu for the next three days, which we both thoroughly enjoyed and I soon forgot about the nasty trip to the vets.

Chapter 15

The House Fire

Becky, Mon and another friend, Yvonne, who lived a bit further up the lane, had been going out on Thursday nights to a horse management course at Plumpton College. Tonight was the last one and they decided they would treat themselves to fish and chips on the way home, although Becky being a vegetarian just had the chips.

Becky arrived home just after 9.30pm and brought with her some chips for Tom and a couple of savloys for Tina and I. They had a very strange texture, but were quite delicious. She chatted with Tom for a bit and then walked Tina and I up to the farm for our last walk before bed. As we reached the farm yard, we heard Joe next door coughing. When I say coughing, it was a really deep cough and he just kept on and on. All of a sudden I could smell a disgusting acrid smoke coming from Joe's direction. Something was very wrong, my hackles went up and I barked. Becky had come to the same conclusion and started running back down to the cottage. She shot through the back door and yelled at Tom to phone the Fire Brigade – "Joe and Mon's house is on fire" she screamed at him.

Tom quickly made the call and joined Becky round at Joe and Mon's front door. "The Fire Brigade are on their way" he reported.

"In hind sight, I knew something was wrong when we got home" said Becky. She looked at Joe "I realise now, what I thought was fog over your house was in fact smoke. It wasn't until I was up at the farm and heard you cough that the penny dropped and I realised it was only foggy above your house".

Joe told them he couldn't get in the back door, the smoke was too thick; so the four of them then discussed what would be cheaper to replace, the thick oak door or the charming leaded light windows. Tom grabbed the sledgehammer from Joe and swung it as hard as he could on the door – it opened, with not too much damage. Joe and Tom had a look around to see if they could work out exactly where the fire was and if it was safe to enter. As they stood there, they could hear the sirens coming down the lane. The fireman luckily had turned up really quickly because the roads were quieter at this time in the evening.

The first fireman on the scene made a quick assessment and shouted loud and clear "Stand back everyone". He went back to the fire engine and grabbed an axe, while everyone scuttled back down onto the lane. The fireman swung the axe over his head and it landed on top of the porch above the now opened door. He swung again and a large chunk of plaster and rubble fell to the floor and immediately a huge flame licked out of the roof. Poor Mon looked really upset. All the lovely things in the house and she couldn't get in to save them.

"Come on" said Becky to Mon, "let's get the tea on for these guys; I think they're going to need it. It won't do to stand here getting upset". "No you're right" Mon replied, her voice quivering. They didn't seem to notice Tina and I sitting on the front lawn. We were watching with wide eyes as the fire crew put on masks and helmets and disappeared into the fire.

The fire chief wanted to know if anyone or any animals were in the house and indeed if there was anything else they should know about. Joe explained the dogs were in the back yard, but he would move them into the stables. "We have a cat called Smokey, but I don't know where she is. We also have a calor gas heater in the lounge and the bottle is quite full".

"Right" said the chief. "The heater is our first priority and then we'll deal with the cat". He rushed over to the front door and shouted to the men already inside about the heater. Seconds later the heater was brought out. A few more seconds later and we heard a couple of burly fireman calling out for the cat "Smokey, Smokey". This seemed to cause some amusement to the rest of the crew and even put a smile on Joe's face.

The firemen had the fire out pretty quickly, but they spent ages checking and double checking everything. They wanted to know what had caused the fire in the first place. The fire chief was confident the fire had started in the airing cupboard which was on the opposite side of the hall from the front door. They were also sure the fire had been started by mice chewing through the electric cables.

It was a long old night; the firemen were still there at 1am in the morning. Tina and I had been called in to bed; so I settled myself in my armchair, where I could still keep an eye on proceedings. Poor Becky and Mon were busy making cups of tea and walking backwards and forwards with trays. The fireman also took it in turns to come into the cottage to collect them, but kept being greeted by Tina barking at them.

Finally at 2am, the firemen went home and Joe and Mon came into the cottage for one more cup of tea. The four of them discussed the whole of the evenings' events and then they too, went to bed. Becky had made up a bed in the spare room in between making all those cups of tea.

I wasn't sure how long I'd been sleeping, but I was woken by Joe crying out "Fire, the roof is on fire!" Apparently, he couldn't sleep and had gone home to check on Joey and Lacey. As he got to the bottom of the cottage drive he heard the crackling. To his horror as he looked at his house, the roof was completely ablaze.

Tom ran downstairs and I heard him calling the emergency services – He was shouting for them to send a fire engine as quickly as they could and gave them the address. Mon and Becky followed quickly behind and were both wriggling into jumpers and coats as fast as they could. Becky hopped out of the back door and nearly fell over while pulling on her wellies. Mon was shouting at Joe as she ran to catch him up "please don't go in the house Joe, wait for the fire brigade, they won't be long"; she was nearly hysterical.

As Tom and Becky reached Joe and Mon, I could tell they were all really upset. There was nothing they could do; the roof was well alight. The flames were 20 foot high and the tiles were exploding as they heated up. The fire brigade were even quicker reaching the cottage the second time around. They'd hardly parked up and it was all action stations. The firemen grabbed the hoses and started shooting great jets of water over the cottage roof. Then there was an all mighty explosion and most of the roof disappeared into the house.

Becky put her arm round Mon as they both stood there and sobbed. I didn't know what to do, I wanted to go to them, but thought perhaps I should stay where I was; like Tom had told me. The ladies soon came my way and went into Becky's kitchen. On went the kettle again.

The firemen were still there at daybreak and the Chief Fire Investigator had turned up. It transpired that Sunflower Cottage had originally been an army barracks in the Second World War. Afterwards, someone had built the picture postcard cottage around it and more importantly had added a second roof. The firemen had thoroughly checked everything after the initial fire, but obviously were unable to detect there was a second roof. The Inspector decided that probably a bird's nest in between the two roofs was smouldering away and eventually set fire to the upper roof.

After the fire crew had gone, the four of them sat in the kitchen and reflected on the nights events. Poor Joe and Mon had lost everything. They just had the clothes they were standing in. Mon was particularly upset about the family photos and the lovely painting of Califfe, her horse, which Joe had had done for a special birthday gift. As was typical of Becky, she gathered together a selection of her and Tom's clothes and assured Mon and Joe they could stay as long as necessary. She laughed as she handed the clothes over "you might need some baler twine to hold things up. Your friends will think you've lost a lot of weight, as Tom and I are obviously a few sizes bigger". It was the first time I heard them laughing, as Mon and Joe thanked Becky. "The main thing is no-one was hurt and I'm sure the rest of the family will help replace some of your photos" said Becky.

The only good thing about all this was that Joe was in the building trade and all his friends pulled together and started rebuilding the cottage within the next few weeks. Joe and Mon bought themselves a caravan and moved into their field. I know Becky and Tom were worried about them as it was bitterly cold that winter, but they seemed happy enough to be there with their animals, as they started to rebuild their lives, bit by bit.

During the following year while the cottage was rebuilt, not much else happened on the farm out of the ordinary. Life pretty much went on in the usual way. The daily routine hardly changed from day to day. The sheep did manage to escape a couple of times, but I soon had them rounded up and back where they were supposed to be. A little more tricky for me to deal with was when the horses escaped and I found them charging around in the field opposite the cottage. Luckily I noticed them and even more lucky for me, they hadn't noticed the gate onto the lane was open.

It was a cold, damp day and I was trying to stay tucked out of the wind; it was ferocious. As not much was happening on the farm, I thought I'd wander down to my armchair and wait for Becky to come home. Just as I was heading into the garage, I saw something golden flash past against the green of the field. I did a double take and realised it was Lady, followed by the rest of the motley gang. They were letting rip; tearing round the field. The wind had no doubt spooked them or was it the excitement of escaping. They all carried their tails high, doing that high knee trot they do and snorting. They were then bucking and kicking their heels in the air and off into a flat out gallop. They looked quite majestic, but I was very wary of going too close when they were in this mood.

I crossed the lane and stood in a crouched position in the gateway. I was frantically thinking how I should deal with this. Firstly, I thought it might be prudent to let them run out of steam before I approached them. This also gave me time to come up with a plan. Finally, they quietened down and began to eat some grass and Lady had her back to me.

I decided Lady was my best bet. If I could persuade her to go back to their field, hopefully the others would follow. I headed out into the field; walking with my head down as low as I could. Every now and then, I broke into a few strides at a jog. As I halved the distance between us, Lady lifted her head and started walking back towards Little Orchards and by chance, the others decided to follow her; what luck. I kept my head low and quickly drew up behind them. Toby was the only one who was keeping an eye on me, but he was still moving forward and keeping up with Lady.

To my amazement, Lady led them down into the yard and went into her stable. Chicory and old Wills then stepped up into theirs and it just left me to encourage Toby into his. I quickly circled and moved into a central position to keep an eye on them. Lady was the first to step forward out of her box, so I barked and moved forward. Thankfully she stepped back. This went on for over an hour before Becky came home from work and came down to check the horses with Tina. She'd been to the field first and was so worried to find the horses' gate was open and they'd gone. Fortunately, she came round to the yard to collect their head collars before going on a hunt for them. I was so relieved to see her.

"Wow" she exclaimed as she came round the corner to find all four horses, not only in the yard, but in their correct stables. "Nipper, you beaut! You are just the best dog. I don't know how you managed that". Well, I'm certainly not going to let on to Becky that Lady put herself in!

Becky soon had Lady and Toby's halters on and led them back to the field. She let Chicory and William follow behind. I received a very welcome pat on the head and loads of "Good Boy's" that afternoon.

By Christmas the following year, Joe and his friends had worked tirelessly to rebuild the new cottage. Mon and Joe were now the proud owners of an absolutely charming new cottage; it was a bit more spacious than the last one, but just as picturesque. They soon had a Christmas tree and decorations up.

Chapter 16

Put That Dog Out!

That Thursday started out as any other. It was a cold frosty February morning. Tom had some good news in the post that morning. He opened the letter and started laughing "Yeah! Wicked!" he exclaimed. I had no idea what he was on about until he delighted in telling Becky when she came home. "We're going to the pub for a meal tonight mate. I just received a cheque from the Tax Man for £600". Becky was laughing too now and gave Tom a hug and kiss. "That's fantastic" she said. "No cooking tonight – hooray!"

As they were getting ready to go out, a friend turned up and stayed for nearly two hours talking. This, as it happens, was fortuitous. After the friend left, Tom and Becky decided to go out the following night. Becky prepared a meal and I found out later, she started to clean some tack in the lounge.

I wandered up to the farm to keep an eye on the sheep and lambs. Nearly all the lambs were born now and the small pens were full up with mums and babies; the heat lamps hanging down from the rafters in the usual way; keeping them warm. There were about 30 'bottle fed' lambs in a separate pen on the right and 3 sickly lambs keeping warm in the office. There were also about 100 cows and calves in the biggest pen on the left of the barn, as I mentioned before.

I snuggled down in my usual spot in the straw and every now and then opened an eye and checked all was as it should be. I'd been there for a couple of hours and gradually became aware that my nose was twitching. I jumped up and sniffed the air "Oh no! Not smoke again!" My blood ran cold. It was smoke; I could see it now as well as smell it. I rushed out of the barn into the cold air and stood at the top of Tom's garden and barked like my life depended on it. "Come on Tom, Becky, Help! Help!"

I ran back into the barn and barked at the sheep "Get out! Save yourselves! Fire! Fire!"

I kept this up for what seemed like ages, running backwards and forwards barking for all my worth. Why can't Tom and Becky hear me and why won't these stupid sheep move themselves. I desperately need help with this.

The sheep eventually realised they were in danger and started calling for themselves. I ran at them barking again and again. "Come on girls, jump out! Run for your lives!"

Finally, Becky turned up in her slippers. "Oh my God, Nipper!" she cried. She ran as near as she could get to the flames and started pulling at the hurdle gates. They wouldn't budge. They were securely tied with baler twine. Becky then realised she needed to move the bales instead. She was grabbing them with one arm and chucking them aside; but there were so many. As she worked her way round the pens, she grabbed the lambs and threw them in with the 'bottle' lambs. The Mums were frantically trying to get in with their babies, but couldn't jump over the hurdles. The bleating and screaming was unbearable. It was difficult to concentrate with all the noise.

Tom ran into the barn and shouted across to Becky "the Fire Brigade are on their way. Be careful and keep an eye on the fire and the roof". He jumped onto the JCB tele-handler which was parked at the front of the barn. Luckily the keys were in it and it started first time. He roared out of the barn, turned right and disappeared round the corner. What's he doing, I thought, we need you in here to help with the sheep; but as the thought went through my head, he was running back in. He headed towards the flames on the left side in between the small sheep pens and the cows. Tom pulled his penknife out of his pocket and was cutting through the baler twine like butter.

The stupid sheep were running everywhere, except to safety; their poor lambs trying to keep up with their mums. They were so confused and frightened. They were running this way and that; out of the barn and then back in.

Tom shouted my name; I looked up to where I thought he was, but I couldn't see him for the smoke. I had to run out of the side of the barn and all the way round to the front of the barn to get to him. I ran through the smoke and bumped into sheep on my way. Luckily Tom shouted again and I bumped into his leg so he knew I was there. "Good boy – Right mate, you're in charge of rounding this lot up and getting them out. Take them round to Becky's side and I'll join you there."

I ran round the back of the sheep and started barking at them again; as I zig-zagged my way towards the fresh air and the main door. Most of the sheep and lambs stayed in front of me, but some were still determined to be stupid and swung round on me and back towards the flames. I carried on regardless and drove the few I had in front of me out of the main door and round towards Becky and the track to the fields. As I got to Becky, I barked to let her know where I was and for her to take charge. I just heard her shout "Good boy" to me, as I spun round and headed back towards Tom to collect some more. I passed Joe and Mon on my way. They had heard the ruckus and had come to help.

By the time I had come back to Becky with another half a dozen, Joe, Mon and Becky were throwing the bottle fed lambs over the six foot fence at the side of the barn. They mingled in with the sheep I was bringing round.

I heard the sirens in the distance and barked to Becky that help was on its way, but I don't think she heard me. She was shouting to Joe and Mon "just keep throwing the lambs out – we'll worry about broken limbs later. We've just got to get them out before the combine catches fire.

Tom had emptied nearly all of the pens on his side of the barn and helped me chase them round to the others. The smoke was definitely getting thicker, the flames were nearly touching the roof and the heat was far more noticeable now. In fact my feet were burning, although I hadn't noticed until now, as my adrenaline was running riot and kept me going.

Tom hadn't realised until then that Joe and Mon had come to help. "Oh thank you guys" he said to them. "Becky, can I leave you in charge of the sheep round here. I've just got a few more to get out and then I'll go back for the cows?"

We never heard Becky's answer. Tom and I ran back into the barn for the umpteenth time, just as two fire engines roared into the yard. The fire chief came in through the main door to assess the situation; followed by several firemen; two of them quickly got geared up and entered the barn armed with huge hoses. I ran on to where the remaining sheep were and barked at them to hurry up and run to the exit.

Tom doubled back and went to talk to the fire chief. "Thank God you're here. Thank you, thank you!" he shouted breathlessly. The noise in the barn was unbelievable. The cows and sheep were all screaming to be let out. The fire had really taken hold and begun to roar in a strange and eerie way. There were now loud cracking sounds coming from the roof. "I've just got a few more sheep to get out and then we've got about 100 cows up there on the left" Tom told him. The fire chief wanted to know what other hazards were in the barn. Tom shouted back to him, as he was heading back towards me and the sheep pens "the combine in the middle; the fertiliser over on the right and the boss's Zephyr car is up at the back on the right. I've taken the gas bottles out and the JCB tele-handler. I can't think of anything else". Tom started coughing as he came back through the smoke to join me. I was running back and forth harassing the sheep, but to no effect. They were so scared. They just stood there bleating; waiting to die.

I caught sight of several men in black uniforms entering the building; one of which was moving forward and spraying water over the straw sheep pens. Suddenly, I heard Tom shout at him, loud and clear "PUT THAT DOG OUT"; as I looked up, Tom was pointing at me. It wasn't only my feet that were burning; Yikes! My coat was on fire. I was completely bowled over as a jet of cold water drenched me and everything around me. I looked up to see a giant of a man swing the hose back onto the burning straw and walk towards the flames. Luckily for me, they arrived just in time. I was instantly back on my feet and back in the thick of it. As I was making my way through the smoke and round the back of the last remaining sheep, I hadn't realised how close I had gone to the flames. Some smouldering straw had fallen on me and caught my coat alight.

Whilst the fireman dealt with me; Tom had finally opened the last of the pens. The sheep were so frightened, they wouldn't move. I probably didn't help when I barked at them to follow me. That's not going to work I thought, so I ran into the pen and got round behind them and barked again. Between Tom dragging them and me hustling them from behind, we eventually managed to get them moving forward and past the flames towards the fresh air. Tom also had three little lambs tucked under his arms.

Tom was really coughing now; he couldn't speak. He just nodded forwards, but I knew where I was going. A couple of fireman were watching Tom struggling to keep the sheep moving forward and came and offered help. "We're taking them out of the front and round to the left to join the others" croaked Tom. We headed round to Becky and delivered the terrified animals. "That's all the sheep out now" coughed Tom. "I'm going back for the cows."

"Please be careful" cried Becky. Becky, Joe and Mon had decided to move all the sheep into Joe and Mon's field; mainly because it had a gate which opened onto the farmyard. I stayed with the sheep and quickly worked out the plan, but Becky thought otherwise. "Nipper, please go with Tom, he needs your help more. We've got this covered here". She looked at me with terrified eyes and pointed towards Tom. I instinctively knew where I had to be.

I scarpered back into the barn and found Tom and stuck close to his side. The smoke was really dense now; we were working completely blind. There were no lights to guide us and anyway, the smoke was stinging my eyes and making them water. Tom felt his way to the gate and the cattle. We could hear the cows mooing at the top far corner of the barn. A couple of fireman with breathing apparatus and torches suddenly appeared by our side. Tom had pulled his jumper up over his face to try and help his breathing. He tried to shout at the fireman to open the gate, but only coughs and croaks came out. He then just pointed and signalled them his intentions and pointed at me and then into the cattle pen. "Okay, understood. Go outside and catch your breath, we'll deal with this". Tom headed towards the back exit, walking, coughing and stumbling, but eventually reached the fresh air and Becky.

"Thank God you're alright! I've been calling and calling you and then asked the fireman to come and find you. I've been so worried" cried Becky.

I barked at the fireman "come on, come on, open the gate and let me in; I'll soon have the cows out". I jumped up into the trough and barked again. The fireman looked to Tom, who was now heading back towards us. He nodded at them "yes, open the gate, let the dog in. I'll open the top gate. You need to send them towards me".

Finally, the gate was opened and I was allowed to do my job. I rushed over to the cows, barking all the time. They were huddled together in the far corner. I could just see their legs under the smoke line. I zigzagged, back and forth and kept on barking to encourage them forward. All of a sudden they stampeded forward out into the fresh air. Tom thankfully had opened the gate. The cows rushed out into the field behind the barn and most of them headed off to the left down the farm track. I ran after them, passing Tom who was still holding onto the gate. They galloped as fast as their legs would take them, along the top of the first field and through the gate into the next field. Luckily all the fields were well fenced and the gate at the bottom on the other side was shut, otherwise who knows where they would have ended up.

Tom found me guarding the entrance to the field they'd ended up in. "Good Boy! You're such a good boy. I don't know what we'd do without you" Tom said, as he pulled the gate shut and double checked the latch had closed properly. "Come on Nipper, let's go and find Becky and the others and check the sheep. We'll come back and check this lot later when they've settled down". We left the cows and calves charging round the field, making quite a hullabaloo.

As we got back to the farm, we found the few cows and calves that had chosen to run in the opposite direction to the main herd. Becky, Joe and Mon had let them in with the sheep. All the animals were making quite a racket, but at least they were now standing still, looking to Tom and me to help them. Tom and Becky had a quick chat which Joe and Mon and decided the best course of action would be to move everything from Joe's field across to the field with the other cows. They were fairly sure that some calves and lambs had been separated from their Mums, so at least they would quieten down if they could be put in together; reunite mums with babies; and more importantly the youngsters could get to some milk.

Just as the decision was made, some of the firemen and locals from the pub, turned up to see if they could help. Apparently, the combine had caught alight, but the flames were now out and they were letting the smoke clear out of the barn. Tom quickly explained his intentions and I was given the important job of going quietly into the field to round up the sheep and the few cows. As Tom opened the gate into Joe and Mon's field, I slunk low and crept round the hedge-line to round up these poor frightened and bewildered animals. Tom, Becky and the others spread themselves out on either side of the gate to fill escape routes. Tom hoped that once we got the cows and sheep moving towards the far field, they would hear the other cows mooing and head towards them. I had to be ready to gather up anything that strayed either way as there were open fields down to main roads flanking both sides of the farm, albeit quite some distance.

The plan nearly worked. We managed between us to head the cows past the farm and they were soon on their way towards the rest of the cattle once they heard the others; but those stupid sheep had other ideas. They followed the cows past the farm, but then swung round to the right and headed across the wide open field with Becky, Mon and a couple of locals in hot pursuit. Now what do I do? I looked at Tom for guidance. "Go, go" he said pointing towards the sheep. Say no more, I was off; doing what I love and do best – running and chasing sheep. As Becky was on the right side of the field, I ran to the left. I didn't look at the sheep; I just sprinted as fast as I could to the bottom of the field to head them off. I was soon way out in front of them and turned sharply across the field and cut across their path. Thank goodness, that worked or I would have looked foolish. The sheep came to an abrupt halt, looked at me and soon realised I was having none of it; they turned and slowly started back towards the farm. "Phew! That was a close one Nipper, well done!" Becky shouted across to me.

As we caught up to Tom and the cows; Tom and Joe were carrying a calf each and walking in front of the cows to encourage them in the right direction. I was amused to see the firemen look down at their spotlessly clean uniforms; look at each other and shrug. They each awkwardly grabbed a calf and were slowly bringing up the rear and now rather dirty. Becky suggested we did the same with the lambs; so everyone grabbed lambs and eventually we had all the animals together in one large field, safe and secure; or so we thought.

We watched in amazement as Mums and youngsters called to each other. The ones that had lost their young were frantically sniffing each lamb or calf and making sure they had the right offspring and vice versa. Lambs and calves were quick to start suckling after all the excitement, probably more for security and reassurance, than hunger. Things eventually quietened down and there were plenty of wagging tails, but Becky was visibly upset as one of the cows and a few sheep were still calling. Tom put his arm round her "it was bound to happen love; it could have been a lot worse. Come on, let's get back to the farm and check the damage".

As we headed back to the farm, all but Becky started chatting away about the terrible events of the evening and their part in the rescue, but it all went quiet again once we entered the barn. It was the smell that hit us first. It was horrible, I won't ever forget it; it made me feel sick to my stomach and I dare say the humans too. The fireman that had come with us, shone their torches round and saw their colleagues were still dousing water over the combine that had indeed caught fire. It was now black and still smoking a bit. I don't think they will be using that again, but they had managed to put out the fire on the straw pens, but it was obvious to me that no-one looked too closely. Tom asked about the boss's Zephyr and Keith, the landlord from the village pub was proud to report that he had managed to drive it out and it was parked further down the drive.

Keith then piped up "there's tea and coffee for everyone down at the cottage – I'm brewing!" Becky thanked him and again thanked everyone for turning up to help. "I really don't know what we would have done without you all". Keith put his arm round her and that was it. The tears rolled down her face and as hard as she tried not too, the sobs started. Mon and Keith led Becky down to the house, followed by a few fireman and their new friends from the pub.

Tom was still in the barn so I went back to find him. He had gone with the fire chief and some of the fireman with torches to check the cow pen. The smoke had now cleared, but it was pitch black and even with the torches it was difficult to see. I wandered into the pen while the men were chatting. It was very feint, but I heard a noise in the far corner, so I moved in for a closer look. To my surprise and happy surprise, there was a calf curled up in the straw. I drew closer to it as it stared back at me; wide-eyed. Poor thing I thought, as I gave it a nudge. I started whining to let Tom know it was here. "What is it boy" asked Tom? I whined louder and nudged the calf again. Tom and the fireman came over to me and Tom knelt down in the straw. "Good boy, good boy Nipper" he said, as he ruffled my head and neck. He said to the calf "I know where you belong little'un, but I think we'll put you in the trailer for the rest of the night and have a vet check you out in the morning. Becky will be thrilled". With that Tom scooped up the calf and made him comfortable in the small horse trailer parked outside.

Tom and one of the firemen then went down into the office and gathered up the three sickly lambs that seemed oblivious to the events of the evening. As Tom passed the fireman a lamb he said "we'll take them down to the house to keep warm, as the electrics have gone off up here. It will hopefully take Becky's mind of other things". "Good idea" replied the fireman, who now had a sad smile on his face, looking pleased to be holding his little bundle.

As we reached the kitchen, everyone was telling tales and recounting their part in the rescue. All agreed it could have been a lot worse and I heard Becky say "we could have lost everything if Nipper hadn't alerted us. I couldn't believe he was actually trying on his own to get the sheep out. How he does it, I don't know. He surely is a dog in a million. Talk of the devil, here come's our star!" I received the biggest hug, as Becky's tears dripped onto my nose. I looked into her eyes and licked her face, in thanks for the appreciation.

Tom also stroked my head and gave me the proudest look. He said nothing, but I knew he was pleased with me. He disappeared into the house and joined the others for a cup of tea. I lay down by the back door for a while, absolutely exhausted and Tina came out to join me. She sniffed round me and begun to gently lick my paws. That felt good, they were so sore. I was pretty exhausted, but there was so much going on in my head, I knew I would not be able to sleep.

Everyone went home about 2am in the morning and the lights went out in the cottage shortly afterwards. I slowly hauled myself up and climbed into my armchair; I might as well be comfortable and at least get some well earned rest.

Chapter 17
Putting Things Back Together

Becky quietly slipped out of the back door about 6am. I was cold, probably because I was so tired. The ground was covered in a heavy frost and it was just starting to get light. I slipped down from my armchair and as my paws met the ground, it was evident actually how sore they were. I followed Becky up to the farmyard and past the barn. We both walked slowly and I wondered where we were going. As we reached the gate to Joe and Mon's field; Becky stopped and had a look round. We both saw it together, a tiny white bundle, tucked in under some brambles. We cautiously made our way over to it and Becky again started to cry. I thought it was dead and probably so did she. "Oh you poor little thing" she sobbed. Most of the wool on its back had been singed by the fire. As Becky bent down to touch it, I too nudged it with my nose. It smelt burnt.

To my surprise, it wasn't dead at all, just in a deep sleep. It let out a small breathe; you could clearly see the vapour in the cold air. "Oh Nipper, it's alive" squeaked Becky. The poor little creature most definitely had had a lucky escape. "Quick have a look round for any more" she said as she picked up the little lamb and started gently rubbing it. We both walked round the edges of the field, but alas, there was only the one. Becky tucked the little miracle into her jacket and we headed off towards the rest of the animals.

As we passed the trailer with the calf in, Becky slowed down and put her finger up to lips "let's not disturb him in there, the vet has to check him over later. We'll give it a wide berth" and she beckoned me to keep close to her.

As soon as we arrived at the gate, three lonely sheep and a few lambs came towards us and started bleating quietly. Becky put the little lamb down on the ground and stepped back. The sheep sniffed every inch of the poor little chap and he sniffed each potential Mum in return. A couple of sheep wandered off and it wasn't long before he found what he was looking for - some milk. He was biffing poor old Mum's belly and before long was suckling and wagging his tail.

Becky talked to the cow that had started mooing in the distance that her calf was fine and they'd be reunited soon. Whether she understood or not, I don't know, but she stopped her mooing as we left the field and headed back to the farm. Again we took a wide berth round the trailer and as we arrived back at the barn, we were greeted by the farm owner, Richard's Dad. It was still really early, but quite a bit lighter now and Becky looked surprised to see him. A bit embarrassed too, as it was obvious she had been crying. She was wiping away tears as she said "Good Morning".

She related some of the night's events and also explained about the lamb we had just found. "I'm not convinced Mum and lamb belong together, but they were both caught in the fire last night. They both have singed coats and probably smell the same to each other. Either way, it's a miracle the little chap survived the cold night on his own and it's lovely to have a happy ending to such a traumatic event. There is one more reunion I'm looking forward to and that's the calf in the trailer and his Mum who's fretting out in the field".

Becky offered Richard's Dad some coffee, but he declined as he had to go to work. He thanked Becky for all that she had done and drove off. Becky picked up three milk bottles from the office and we returned to the cottage. Minutes later I had an extra-large bowl of porridge brought out to me and I was joined by Tina who had the same. "You can both eat outside this morning, while I give the lambs their bottles in here" said Becky and shut the back door. Tina asked me how my paws were in between mouthfuls. "Still sore, but a lot better for you licking them clean last night" I replied.

The Weasel arrived at the cottage and Tom came out to meet him. Will shook Tom's hand and thanked him for all his efforts on saving his sheep. I hadn't realised until then that they were actually his sheep; I always thought they belonged to the farm; not that it matters; they're still stupid sheep. Tom went on to explain to Will that he would have lost the lot had it not been for me. "First priority this morning is to call the vet. Nipper's paws need to be checked; he was running round on burning embers, not that I think he noticed. He didn't notice his coat was on fire until the fireman had to turn the hose on him. There are also a few of the sheep and lambs that need checking over. I'm afraid some may have suffered burns and possibly have damaged lungs because of the smoke. I'm also really sorry to report that we did lose a few. I can honestly say they didn't suffer; the smoke got them, it was so thick. I haven't had the courage to look just yet. I just couldn't get near enough to them because …" Tom broke off. He looked tired and shaken and I'm sure those were tears in his eyes.

Will put his hand on Tom's shoulder in a friendly gesture and told him "don't you worry about that mate; the least I can do is sort that side of things out. I think you and Becky have done enough. If it's alright with you, I'll wander up and have a look round on my own. Perhaps you could call the vet and put the kettle on. I'll be back down in a minute."

Tina and I had finished our porridge, so followed Will up to the farm, but at a distance, more because I couldn't walk too fast. As we reached the entrance of the barn, Tina hesitated. She was taken aback by the smell. "What's that awful smell?" Tina asked me. "I think it's a mixture of burnt and wet straw and I'm afraid to tell you, a few of the sheep and lambs didn't make it out last night. I feel really bad about it; I did my best. They just wouldn't listen to me. I feel I've let Tom and Becky down; they are both so sad this morning".

Tina moved closer to me and looked me in the eyes "Nipper, from what I hear, none of animals would have got out alive if you hadn't called for help. Tom and Becky think the world of you. They're not upset with you mate. I think they are just tired and a bit upset about the sheep. All I know is that everyone thinks you're a hero and so do I. As you said, you did your very best; no-one can ask more than that."

We stood and watched the Weasel walk over to where the sheep pens had been. He stopped and shook his head; he then moved on and looked in dismay at the burnt-out combine. He was there only seconds and passed us as he marched back down to the cottage. He called out to Tom and entered the kitchen. "That's a right old mess up there. You'll need to dig a big hole for the sheep; put them in the top corner of the field behind the barn and I'd like it done before the vet gets here. What time's he coming?"

I could sense Tom's hackles go up as he snapped back at Will. "The vet's on his way, he'll be here in about two hours. He's giving us time to sort ourselves out. As for your sheep, you'll have to find someone else to bury them. I'm sorry, but I'm not doing that."

The Weasel didn't get his cup of coffee. Tom walked straight past him and headed up to the farm. Tina and I were hot on his heels. He was definitely upset, I would even say angry. Jim, the new farm-hand, had just arrived for work and Tom went over to talk to him. Jim had started on the farm a few weeks ago and Tina and I both really liked him; he really understood how to treat us animals.

Tom began giving Jim a step by step account of all the horrors from the previous night. They then started to discuss what needed to be done this morning. The Weasel came up behind them and wanted to know what was going on. "Well, who's going to bury the sheep then? – it needs to be top priority" Will spat out. Jim spoke quietly and volunteered "I'll do it; you really can't expect Tom to do that from the sound of things."

Before the Weasel could say another word, Tom told him he was going to rig up some pens at the back of the barn and bring the animals back in for the vet to check over. "We'll need to sort them out as they come back in. Unfortunately, they're all in together in the second field out the back. Jim and Becky can help us walk them back from the field.

The other thing we need to organise is some food for them all. The silage in the trough will need to be emptied out; as it will stink of smoke and the cows won't want that. The sacks of nuts should be alright for the sheep though.

I think we'll find the animals that need checking over will be obvious when we see them and we also need to locate the half dozen sheep that are yet to lamb. We also mustn't forget the calf in the trailer." With that Tom headed off to the back of the barn.

The three men got to work in silence. I went with Tom and Will who started shifting the hurdles around to make up a gangway to lead the sheep through for the vet and a small pen for after. Tom went over to the cattle pen to shut the gate when we suddenly heard him cry out "I don't believe it!" We all looked in his direction. "Hello little fellow. You poor thing. Have you been here on your own all this time?" I wandered over and there in the far corner was a small black calf buried in the straw. How on earth did we all miss him last night? I was sure we'd checked they were all out. Tom said to Will "I feel bad we missed finding him last night, but at least he looks no worse for wear. I think he must be in shock. We'd better ask the vet to check him over too."

Will smiled at Tom and told him "it's no surprise you didn't find him the dark; he's almost jet black and buried himself in the lovely straw bed you've given them."

About an hour past and Becky turned up with a tray of coffee and some hot bacon sandwiches.

"Thought you might need some sustenance" she said in a cheery voice. "Can I help? I've phoned work and they are fine with me having the day off today." Tom was pleased to report to her about the calf and it certainly seemed to cheer her mood from this morning.

It wasn't long before they had things organised in the barn and Tom called Jim to ask if he could help round up the animals for the vet's visit and we were on our way to retrieve them from the field.

The timing was excellent. Just as we had returned the sheep and cows to their relevant pens, the vet turned up. I've seen this vet several times. A tall, serious man; he didn't talk much to the men, but was always kind to me. He would barely mumble "Good Morning" to the chaps, but he'd chat away to me and enquire how I was and he always remembered my name. He just listened intently to the symptoms given by Will or Tom and only spoke to ask questions about the patient. We would watch him scratch his head or rub his chin in silence; you could almost see him thinking, but I knew Tom and Will thought he was just the best vet and had much respect for him.

This morning was no different. He politely greeted Tom and Will with a barely audible "Good Morning" and then came straight to me. "Hello Nipper – How are you? I hear you've been in the wars. We'll soon have you sorted out. Now let's have a look at those paws and check your breathing".

I lay down while he applied some greasy, but soothing, stuff on my paws and instructed Tom. "Apply liberally; twice a day or when you think he needs it. For instance; he may need extra applications if he's paws get wet. I've checked his breathing and he seems fine. I'm amazed considering what you tell me he went through and from the looks of his coat, Nipper was jolly lucky". He placed his hand under my chin and gently lifted my head while he looked me in the eyes and told me what a good and brave boy I'd been. "I always knew you were special; the courage of a lion" he told me for everyone to hear. He then rubbed between my ears. "Right, whose next?"

Will suggested the vet check the calves next, so they could be put back out in the field; out of the way. Tom gathered up the little black calf and brought him forward for the vet to check over. The vet gave him a good examination and listened to his chest with some thin rubber tubes that were hanging round his neck. Everyone went quiet and waited to hear the result. "Nought wrong with him. Probably a little shocked, but more likely tired and hungry" the vet reported. With that a big black cow behind us let out a very loud "moo", to which the calf replied equally loudly and set off in her direction. Tom was quick to scope the calf up and clambered over the pen and let the calf go. I noticed Becky wipe away a tear as Mum and calf touched noses. Mum licked her boy's face and pushed him towards her udders for a drink. "That's one happy calf" said the vet with a big grin on his face – the first smile I'd seen from him – ever.

There was also nothing wrong with the calf that spent the night in the trailer and he too was pleased to be returned to his Mum. Next the vet checked over the sheep. He painstakingly listened to all of them and Tom and Will separated the ones that were alright into one big pen and the sheep that needed further treatment into the smaller pen in between the cow pen and the others.

Now came the turn of the sheep and lamb that had noticeably burnt coats and had had an emotional reunion earlier on this morning. I could see the vet was sad to see the state of them and was particularly gentle when handling them. "I'm amazed these two have survived" he reported. "Sheep are renowned for giving up and dying for a lot less than they've been through; but I'm pleased to report, that although Mum is a little wheezy, the lamb is fine, they should make it. I'll give you some crystals to add to Mum's food to help with her breathing. As Becky and I guided them to their new pen, Richard's Mum, Peggy turned up. I'd known Peggy my whole life. I think she had a soft spot for me, but she also loved all the other animals.

"I just wanted to come and see how things were going and thank you all for your help last night. How are the animals fairing? I've been so worried about them, but I see you've got it all in hand" she enquired. Tom filled her in on the vet's report so far and that there were just half a dozen left to check, albeit, the sheep that the vet was checking now, had unfortunately been caught in the fire and had some serious blisters to her back side. This was particularly worrying, as she had yet to give birth. As Tom and Peggy watched, the vet gently applied some cream to her burns, when she suddenly went into a sort of spasm and if I didn't know better, it looked like she was about to push a lamb out.

But that is exactly what was happening. The vet called out "Good timing! I can see two little feet! Can someone hold her front end? Before I could blink, there in the vet's arms was a little wet lamb, all covered in mucus. The vet started clearing the sticky stuff away from its mouth and nose. He then took hold of it by the back legs and swung it gently to and fro to aid its breathing. It jolted into life with a violent wriggle and a gasp. The vet nearly dropped it, but just managed to guide it down safely in front of Mum's nose. She started the maternal licking of her lamb clean to loads of "Oos" and "Ahhs" from everyone watching. Then all went silent around me and as I looked round, everyone was smiling, but wiping the odd tear from the corners of their eyes. For the life of me, I don't understand these humans at all – it's just another lamb – isn't it?

As the vet stood up he said "Isn't nature amazing. "We're all standing here thinking that was going to be painful. We humans put far too much emotional attachment to these things. Animals just get on with it."

Peggy then quipped back "I'd like to see a man just get on with it like that, especially with such a big lamb and a burnt behind!" Everyone started laughing; even the men were nodding their heads in the realisation of how right she was. The vet replied "Okay, point taken!"

He paused and spoke again "Well, my job is done here today. Any problems at all, just phone me, day or night. I would also like to say, you were jolly lucky. All of you must remember this day; put it down to experience. You must hold fast to the thought that this was the day you saved all those cows and sheep – not the day you lost some". I could see everyone nodding their heads. Tom and Will shook his hand and thanked him, followed by Peggy and Becky. The vet came over to me and gave my head another rub, before driving off.

Chapter 18

I'm Honoured

A car pulled up in the drive just after lunch. A smart young man climbed out carrying a very impressive camera. "Hello guys – where's your Mum?" he asked me and Tina. She went into protect mode and was barking aggressively at him, but he didn't seem perturbed as he passed her to the kitchen door. I wondered who he was and why he was here. I never imagined for one minute how my life was about to change and that many new adventures were about to unfold.

Becky came out to meet him and they shook hands. He introduced himself as the photographer from the local paper and thanked Becky for phoning his colleague, Sarah, with the story about me. "Thank you for coming" Becky said. "This is the brave and courageous Nipper I rung Sarah about. I have also asked her to do a general 'Thank You' to the Fire Brigade and everyone else who came to our rescue last night.

They chatted at length, while he pointed the camera in my direction and clicked away. I had to sit and pose this way and that and then have some photos taken up in the barn with the sheep behind me; I really quite enjoyed being centre of attention.

A couple of days later, Becky told me while we were out on a walk, that reporters had starting phoning for details of the dog that saved the animals. More photographers started turning up and there was even a call in the early hours of the morning from a reporter on the other side of the World in Australia. The following day, a very excited Becky came home from work armed with several newspapers. Apparently, her Mum and Dad had read about my exploits in the Daily Telegraph and several friends had rung Tom and Becky to say likewise in all the main newspapers.

By the end of the week a film crew arrived armed with huge cameras and tripods and they wanted to film me at work. I could sense the excitement from Tom, Becky and even the Weasel, as Richard was nominated, as the farm owner's son, for the filming for the 'South Today' programme to be shown on a television. All Richard and I had to do was herd some sheep. I found this all jolly amusing, by the time they'd got the film they wanted, even the sheep were excited too and I was shown on News at 10 and another television programme, South Today, racing round the field herding sheep. Nobody had told me where I was supposed to be herding them to, so we just kept going round in circles, faster and faster on every lap.

The elderly couple up the lane, a brother and sister, Jim and Elsie, came down with a box of doggy biscuits for me. Jim slowly walked his old Jack Russell past the cottage every day, come rain or shine, and returned carrying a bundle of twigs under his arm for their log fire; their only form of heating.

Tom and Becky had noticed this, so at the beginning of last winter, took a tractor bucket load of logs round and dropped them over the fence. Jim and Elsie obviously thought one kindness deserved another and I was very grateful to them.

Parcels started arriving via the postman, again boxes and boxes of treats from all over the country; which, of course, I shared with Tina. Then there was a special parcel which unfortunately wasn't edible. The postman knocked on the door and Tom had to sign for it. After he'd opened it, he came outside to show me. "Look Nipper, a lady from Yorkshire saw your photo in the paper and was so touched by your story, she asked her husband to paint your picture. Don't you look handsome – how very posh, you've been painted in oils. Becky's going to love this".

Things just started to calm down and life began to go back to normal. It was a lovely spring day when I was woken early for my walk, but unusually after breakfast I was meticulously groomed. I wondered what on earth was going on. Tom and Becky invited me into their car, both looking very smart and off we went. I had no idea where we were going and it was a lot further away from the farm than I'd been before.

We pulled up into a large car park set in front of a big old building with RSPCA Head Quarters in bold letters marked up on the wall. As I was let out of the car on a lead, there were several people there that I knew and oddly enough, a couple of lambs; also on leads. Both Tom and Becky's parents were here and Tom's sister Lesley and the kids and many others. Now I really was wondering what was happening, but everyone seemed relaxed and jolly, so I presumed there was nothing to worry about. A nice lady came out to greet us and led us into the back garden, where I was presented with an award in the shape of a shield from a man called Paul Darrow. He apparently was a famous actor who played 'Avon' on the televisions 'Blake Seven'. The Plague was accepted by Tom and it read 'For Intelligence and Courage'. Everyone clapped and more photos were taken of me and the lambs and then everyone tucked into some sandwiches and cakes and either drunk tea or lemonade. Tina was a bit miffed at being left on her own for a while when we arrived home. I didn't dare tell her about the cakes.

A few weeks later I was groomed up again. While Becky was brushing my coat, I sensed she was not in the best of moods. She chatted away and kept apologising to me, but I didn't understand what for. "I'm sorry mate, you've got to go to London; it's not right, they should come to you. They shouldn't expect a country animal to be happy in the town. Don't you be scared now; Will has promised to look after you; I just wish I could come too. I'm so sorry; I feel I've let you down, but you'll be home before you know it."

So you can imagine my concern when I was asked to jump into the back of the Weasel's car. His wife was there though and she certainly seemed pleasant enough and I heard her promise Becky and Tom she would take great care of me and look after me every step of the way. "What way? Where are you taking me?" I wanted to know. It was a big estate car and so I lay down and hid behind the seat in the hopes they would forget I was there. The journey went on forever; I felt a long way from home. I could see out of the windows, building after building passing by; this was foreign territory for me. I was just thinking that I would need to let them know I needed to relieve myself, when we pulled into a car park and I was let out of the car. I searched for a bush or tree, but in the end had to settle for the nearest lamppost and did the necessary. As I looked up, there was a huge building that went up to the sky and on the front of it was 'BBC'.

We walked along miles of corridors and went up in a lift, a very strange sensation, eventually arriving in a very well lit studio. It was very hot in there, probably because of all the lights and again there were loads of cameras; but this time on wheels. I was soon put at my ease when I saw another dog sitting quietly next to a man and a lady and was constantly being stroked and pampered. I wanted to go and introduce myself, but I had to wait around for ages until eventually I was lead over to a bench and introduced to Peter Duncan and his delightful Golden

Retriever named Goldie. She was very welcoming and seemed very relaxed, which put me at my ease. Both of us were fussed over, even the Weasel stroked me constantly. Will sat down on a large sofa and chatted with Peter and I heard my name mentioned several times, as Will again repeated all that I had done on the night of the fire. Peter handed Will a 'Blue Peter' Badge which he was obviously very pleased with. Apparently we were on the Blue Peter Show that all the children watch when they come home from school.

We were only in the building for a couple of hours and then it was back in the car and heading home. I had another great day being centre of attention. All the kind people in the building wanted to stroke and pat me and best of all, the Weasel and his wife stopped for fish and chips on the way home and shared some with me.

On arriving home I had the best greeting from Tina and Becky; they were so pleased to see me and wanted to know all about my day. Will told Becky he was sure I had actually quite enjoyed myself – "no harm done. Oh, Nipper likes fish and chips". Becky smiled and I could tell she was relieved to have me home.

I was groomed again a few weeks later and again wondered what was going on. This time I went in the car with Becky, but this time, not too far away, in fact just the next village. It was the Hurstpierpoint Summer Fair and all I had to do was trot round the main ring as crowds of people clapped and cheered as I was lead round. There was a booming voice echoing round the ground. I never did pinpoint where the noise was coming from, but a man was singing my praises and telling everyone about the night I saved the cows and sheep from the fire. Several of the children wanted to stroke me and again I had to have my photo taken with this child and that. Becky was very pleased when they handed her a basket of flowers and I had jolly good fun too. I met loads of other lady friends; a few even looked like me, although Becky wouldn't let me chat with them for long.

The leaves on the trees were just starting to turn golden and most mornings started misty and were often quite chilly; autumn was on the way.

Our next jaunt out was to Lewes Sheep Dog Trials. Again I was brushed and groomed to perfection. My white chest nearly sparkled and I felt all lovely and clean. Today though, Becky stopped on the journey at Tom's Mum and Dad's house where we picked up Tom's brother, Daniel. After saying our goodbyes to Tom's parents, we were in the car for about half an hour with Daniel reading some instructions on how to get wherever we were going. We pulled into a farm with the most stunning views. We were quite high up looking over field upon field that lay before us. I felt right at home, there were sheep and collie dogs everywhere. Some of the dogs were already working, but most were lying around patiently, awaiting their turn. As I watched, I noticed that the other dogs were doing the same thing over and over again. They seemed to be taking it in turns to run the sheep through a course of gates and hurdles. The men and women working them were using whistles and calls that I haven't heard in a long time. I was just wondering when it was going to be my turn when Becky and Daniel lead me over to some people in a tent and introduced us. Becky had been invited to give out the awards to the winners of the sheep dog trials. I have to say, I was really disappointed. I was busting to show off my skills, but apparently this was not to be.

Late in the afternoon, when the last dog had run the course; all the men, women and dogs gathered together for the prize giving. Becky and I were introduced to the crowd that had gathered and once again I heard my name mentioned and everyone started clapping and cheering. Becky was handed a card with everyone's signatures and a red rosette for me. The rosette read 'Award for Courage' and the card had a picture of a collie. Becky was beaming from ear to ear and thanked everyone on my behalf. Again they all made a real fuss of me and I was sorry when we had to go home.

Becky told me the following day that we had made the front page of the Evening Argus newspaper and what a good boy I was. I presumed this would be the last of our trips out, but I was wrong. The best was yet to come.

On a very cold winter's day, once more I was groomed up and taken in the car with not only Tom and Becky, but this time Richard and Avril and Richard's sister Liz came too. This trip felt different. Whether it was the jollity in the car on the journey or perhaps I was getting used to leaving the farm, I don't know. We were back up in London again in no time and Tom, Becky and the others were certainly very excited about something; so naturally, I felt excited too. We pulled up into a hotel car park in the dark and I had absolutely no idea where we were. As I was lead through the main door of the Grosvenor Suite, I noticed how very grand and posh it all looked. We were shown into this enormous room. There were several chairs surrounding several tables which were all laid out in a most spectacular way. Everything was glinting in the light.

Almost immediately we were brought tea and sandwiches and the guys were instructed on the order of events. While they shared their sandwiches with me; a lady arrived with a sweet little dachshund cross dog called Toby. He could not be confused with the giant of a horse, back at the farm. This Toby, was about the size of one of big Toby's hooves. He and I struck up a rapport straight away. He was a little nervous and wondering, as was I, what on earth was going on. Once the tea was drunk and the sandwiches polished off, Toby and I were asked to jump up on one of the velvet covered chairs at one of the splendid tables. Toby was duly lifted onto his chair and once I realised what was expected, I jumped onto mine. Toby's owner was then asked to stand Toby up on his hind legs, on account of his size, with his front paws on the table so that the photographers could actually see him. Unfortunately, I misunderstood and thinking they wanted me to do likewise, I rather over did it. It was their fault. The photographers on the other side of the table were all calling my name and in my excitement, I leapt onto the table and headed towards them. Knives, forks, spoons, expensive cut glasses and candelabra went flying in all directions to the background of Tom, Becky, Richard, Avril and Liz all hollering at me in unison to "get down/stop/stay!"

I stopped dead in my tracks before they shouted again. Everyone grabbed glasses, the fallen and those left standing. A staff member from the hotel picked up the candelabra and I was duly summoned back to my chair. I looked in Tom's direction and apologised with my eyes. "Not your fault Nipper. It's alright, nothing broken. Now just stay right there for your photo there's a good boy" Tom said reassuringly. Becky, Avril and Liz started giggling, which reassured me I was forgiven.

The girls went off to change into evening dresses and looked absolutely stunning on their return. If they hadn't still been giggling, I might not have recognised them. Richard and Tom then lead me out to another room where there were dogs galore; all shapes and sizes, but all locked up in cages. Tom said he wouldn't be long and to behave myself as I was handed over to a couple of charming girls who had volunteered to look after me and Toby while everyone had dinner. The girls took us out for a short walk and Toby and I agreed we were lucky not to have been put in a cage.

On returning, my attention was drawn to lovely looking white poodle just a little way away from us. He didn't look too happy though. His guardian had him standing on a table and was ferociously grooming him, not in the kind, relaxing way Becky groomed me. His owner was yanking at his coat with a thin metal comb, time and time again. It looked painful. Then, all of a sudden, he let out a yelp. The owner didn't apologise to him for her mistake, instead she tapped his nose with the metal comb and growled at him to be quiet. I winced for him. She did this several more times before Tom, Becky and Toby's owner came to collect us. As luck would have it, the poodle yelped once more as we walked past. Tom glared at the owner as she brought the comb down on the poor poodle's nose. "That's not fair" said Tom to the owner. She totally ignored him. "We'll see about that" said Tom to Becky. I was lead round until Tom found someone who looked in charge and reported the treatment of the poodle.

We then went back to the ball room and took our seats; well I sat on the floor under the table and Toby sat on his Mum's lap. We watched and listened to the people talking up on the stage and then Becky and I were invited up with Toby and his owner. A man introduced a very smart lady, who obviously everyone knew, to present the awards. She was introduced as Katie Boyle and her little poodle 'Bizzie Lizzie', who had been rescued from the Battersea Dogs Home. He then went on to tell everyone about how my new friend, Toby, had sniffed out a gas leak on his walk before bed and kept barking at a certain spot. His owner took him home, but he started to scratch the door and went straight back to the same spot and barked some more. His owner knew this was unusual behaviour and could now smell the gas herself. She phoned the emergency services and several people were evacuated from the flats. The Emergency Services felt sure Toby had saved a lot of lives, as they worked to repair a gas leak that could have had serious consequences. Toby's owner was presented with a 'Life Saving Award' on Toby's behalf. She looked thrilled when the audience began applauding. The man then went on to tell my story and presented Becky with a 'Devotion to Duty Award'. Becky looked pleased to hear the same clapping and cheering and patted and stroked me fondly.

Another dog was then brought up the stairs onto the stage. He had the biggest paws and the largest, most expressive eyes I've ever seen. His name was Oscar and he was a German Wirehaired Pointer. He knew he was handsome and he oozed with personality. He won the Pro-Dogs Gold Medal Award for Pet of the Year. Apparently Oscar was quite famous, often seen on the television and helped raise a lot of money for charity. He, like me, used to open fetes and such like. More importantly though, he used to spend hours visiting children in hospital. The parents of a 12 year old boy, Neil, who was in a coma, knew their son loved Oscar, so they begged Oscar's owner to come and visit him. Oscar and his owner spent a long time visiting Neil; when Oscar decided to gently nudge the boy. "Oscar!" exclaimed Neil, as he opened his eyes and smiled.

After more clapping and cheering had died down, the other dogs that we'd seen in the room with the cages were being led into the ball room. They were paraded round by their owners. We were told by the man on the stage that they had all won Obedience Competitions or done something else special, but where was the large white poodle? I looked around, but he was nowhere to be seen. Tom noticed he was absent too and mentioned it quietly to Becky and the others. "It looks like the lady with the poodle has been sent home in disgrace" said a smiling Tom.

As if the day couldn't get more exciting, we were whisked off in a taxi to the Kensington Hilton Hotel; this was even more luxurious than where we'd come from. The talk in the taxi was that we were going to stay overnight and Becky and I were to appear on 'Breakfast Time' early tomorrow morning. The BBC were paying for two rooms for us and two rooms for Toby and his owner and her brother. It was nearly midnight and I was long overdue for a sleep, but I could sense a buzz from the others and that the night had just begun.

As soon as we were booked into the hotel, Richard, Avril, Tom and Becky decided to go for a drink and something to eat; hadn't they eaten enough all ready? Anyway, I was given my own special doggy passport and lead into a back room where a couple of very nice ladies were delighted to meet me and offered to look after me, as I wasn't allowed in the dining room. One of them disappeared and came back with a plate of very delicious chicken bits that she had begged off the chef. I licked the plate clean, put a paw on the lady's lap to say thank you and while she stroked my head, I lay down beside her chair. I think I was asleep before my eyes closed.

The next thing I remember was Tom and Richard waking me to take me out for a walk before bed. We walked past a few buildings as they searched for a patch of grass for me, when we came to a building with a long, but short wall. I couldn't see over it, but

Tom and Richard told me to jump over. "Perfect spot" said Richard, "HM Revenue and Customs' front lawn". Tom and Richard were giggling like I'd never heard them before. I quickly relieved myself and jumped back. I didn't understand what they were laughing at, but they laughed all the way back to the hotel, so I wagged my tail and pretended I understood.

I was led up the stairs by Tom and Becky and we entered a huge bedroom with the biggest bed I've ever seen. They sorted themselves out and got into the bed, laughing about losing each other in the night. Then to my amazement they invited me up on the bed with them. "Really", I thought; "I'm allowed up there on the furniture, but you told me off when I jumped on the table". They didn't need to ask me twice; I leapt from where I was standing and plonked myself straight between them. We all snuggled down and went to sleep. I wasn't asleep for long though; Tom's breathing was so loud. Becky woke him twice to tell him to stop snoring. Then before I knew it, the telephone was ringing with an early morning call from hotel reception.

Tom and Richard walked me back round to the HM Revenue and Customs' front lawn, where I was encouraged to once more jump over the wall. I didn't like to make a mess on the smart lawn, but I didn't have much choice. Tom started laughing and suggested to Richard that they should leave a note of apology for the gardener. On arriving back at the hotel, I was again taken to the telephone room where I was provided with a huge bowl of creamy porridge by the nice lady I saw last night. I suspect Becky had something to do with this. No sooner than I finished eating, Tom and Richard came to collect me and we were once more whisked away in a taxi. We arrived at a building I recognised; I'd been here before for the Blue Peter Show, so I felt quite at home. As we pulled into the car park there were loads of people milling about and cheering. I was well used to the sound of clapping and cheering, but actually this time it wasn't for me. The celebrations were for a famous cricketer called Ian Botham; he had just completed a long walk from John O'Groats and had raised a staggering amount of money for charity.

We joined in with the crowd for a short while until we had to head into the BBC building and introduce ourselves at the reception desk. We were taken upstairs in a lift and asked to wait in a large comfortable room, where we were provided with coffee and biscuits. Good job we didn't eat them all, because Mr Botham and the other walkers joined us in the waiting room not five minutes later; much to the excitement of Tom and the others. He was such a kind gentlemen and seemed interested to meet me and find out why we were there. Considering how famous he was and the amazing effort he'd made to raise so much for the Leukaemia Charity, we were all impressed with his kindness.

A lady came in and told Becky it was time to go for 'make up'. She was gone for some fifteen minutes and when she returned, she was grinning from ear to ear. "Guess who I've just been sitting next to while they made my face up?" she bubbled over. Before anyone could guess, Becky blurted out "only Russell Grant!"

Becky was starting to get nervous or was it excitement? Anyway we didn't have to wait long, the lady returned and requested Toby and his owner and Becky and I to follow her. We went into the room next door. The room had a large window and was very bright from all the spotlights. There were more of those large cameras on wheels and we were invited to sit on the sofa opposite Selina Scott, who was going to interview Becky and Toby's owner. She chatted with us and put Becky at her ease, all the time stroking me. Toby again sat on his owner's lap.

The camera was rolling and Selina invited Becky to explain what I had done to earn my awards. Becky's voiced was quivering as she told Selina how I had alerted her and Tom to the fact that something was very wrong on the night of the fire. She went on to say that I was usually bringing the sheep back into the barn, but not on this occasion. I had risked my life trying to get the sheep out on my own before help arrived. "Nipper is a dog in a million. Collies are known for their intelligence, but he is more than that; he works things out for himself. I have to tell you, we could have lost 300 plus animals on that night, if not for his bravery. It would be so natural for an animal to run from fire, but Nipper not only stayed, he was desperately trying to free the animals; he even caught fire himself and the firemen had to put him out. We are all so proud of him. Becky gave me a hug and I could tell she was near to tears. Selina smiled and nodded her approval to Becky as she thanked her and again stroked me. She then turned to Toby's owner and introduced her.

I was glad to be heading home. All this sitting around was somehow exhausting. I longed to be with Tina and romp round the garden or go for long walks and run through the fields with my ears blowing back in the breeze. As much as it was fun to sleep on that huge bed with Tom and Becky, I was also looking forward to my armchair and the freedom of coming and going as I pleased.

We collected Tina from Tom's sister, Lesley's house and as soon as we arrived back at the farm, Becky took Tina and I down to Little Orchards to see the horses. Tina delighted in telling me she'd had a lovely time at Lesley's, but was pleased to be back home. She quizzed me on where I'd been, but I decided to simply tell her, "Oh, nowhere special, you wouldn't have liked it. I missed you too and I am more than happy to be at home and free again."

Day to day life soon went back to normal and preparations for Christmas began all over again. We saw a lot more of Richard and Avril and I soon put all my adventures behind me and was looking forward to the next. The next being that Richard and Avril were to be married in a couple of months and were moving into the adjoining cottage. Tom and Becky were really looking forward to having them as neighbours. The best bit of news was that the Weasel was leaving the farm, in fact he was packing his things and moving out at the weekend.

The next time I heard about the night of the fire was on Christmas day, when Tom and Becky returned from his sisters. Becky couldn't wait to tell me as she jumped out of the car. "Nipper, look! You really are famous. A well-known celebrity has written about you in his book. It's called 'True Animal Tails'. You're under the section headed 'Bravest of the Brave'. How about that mate?"

The only other time I heard mention of the rescue, were Sunday afternoons when families walked down the lane. Mums often pointed to me and tell their children "that's the famous Nipper, who won a Blue Peter Badge for saving all the sheep and cows from the fire". I'd make a point of sitting up tall and wagging my tail in acknowledgement.

It's said that a dog is man's best friend. Well, that's all I've ever wanted in life; to be everybody's friend and work to the best of my ability, but in return I would hope to be treated fairly and have the security of the pack; I'm more than happy if you wish to be 'Alpha' Dog. Oh! Regular 'walkies', as you call them, regular meals would be good too, especially, if there's an odd cake corner! I've certainly had all of that and more, here at Cherry Tree Farm. Life just couldn't get any better than this.

Printed in Great Britain
by Amazon